GREATER

WATERBURY

A REGION REBORN

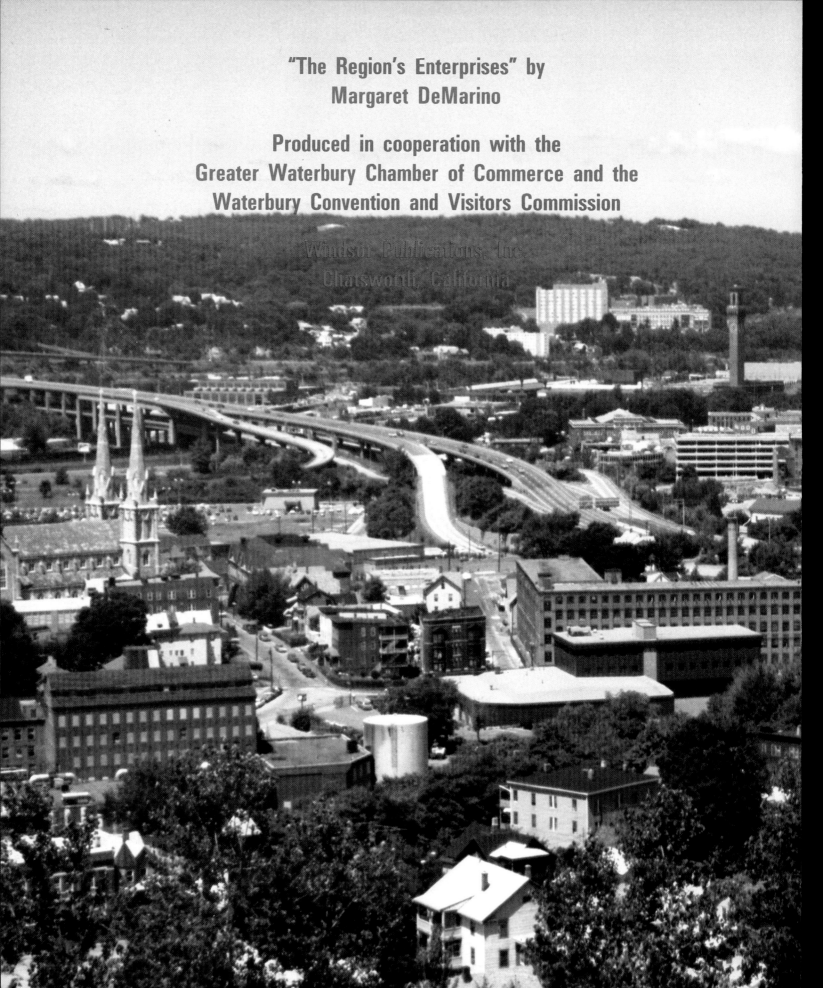

"The Region's Enterprises" by
Margaret DeMarino

Produced in cooperation with the
Greater Waterbury Chamber of Commerce and the
Waterbury Convention and Visitors Commission

Windsor Publications, Inc.
Chatsworth, California

GREATER
WATERBURY
A REGION REBORN

A Contemporary Portrait By **CHARLES MONAGAN**

Windsor Publications, Inc.—
History Books Division
Managing Editor: Karen Story
Design Director: Alexander E. D'Anca

Staff for *Waterbury*
Manuscript Editor: Lane A. Powell
Photo Editor: Loren Prostano
Production Editors: Jeffrey Reeves, Susan L. Wells
Senior Editor, Corporate Profiles: Judith Hunter
Senior Production Editor, Corporate Profiles: Phyllis Gray
Customer Service Manager: Phyllis Feldman-Schroeder
Editorial Assistants: Kim Kievman, Michael Nugwynne,
    Kathy B. Peyser, Theresa Solis
Publisher's Representative, Corporate Profiles:
    Hannah Dresser
Layout Artist, Corporate Profiles:
    Mari Catherine Preimesberger-Powell
Layout Artist, Editorial: Michael Burg
Designer: Ellen Ifrah

Library of Congress Cataloging-in-Publication Data:
Monagan, Charles A.
    Waterbury: a region reborn: a contemporary
portrait/by Charles Monagan
    p. cm.
    "The region's enterprises, by Margaret DeMarino": p.
    Bibliography: p.
    Includes index.
    ISBN 0-89781-317-0
    1. Waterbury (Conn.)—Industries—History.
2. Waterbury (Conn.)—Manufactures—History.
3. Waterbury (Conn.)—Economic conditions.
I. DeMarino, Margaret. II. Title.
HC108.W4M65   1989   89-9065
338.09746'7—dc20   CIP

Windsor Publications, Inc.
Elliot Martin, Chairman of the Board
James L. Fish III, Chief Operating Officer
Michele Sylvestro, Vice-President, Sales/Marketing

THIS PAGE: A crisp winter scene, white snow against a crystal blue sky. Photo by Jack McConnell

FRONTISPIECE: A bright blue sky crowns this Waterbury skyline. Courtesy, Waterbury Convention and Visitors Commission

Contents

Prologue

In Greater Waterbury, the first light of day strikes the peak of Todd Hill in Bethlehem, the region's highest point, and then it works its way down, flooding the many lower hills with a renewing light.

The sunlight illuminates such lofty symbols of the area's rich New England past as Good Hill in Woodbury, from which a tired band of settlers in 1673 first laid eyes on the fertile Pomperaug Valley; Spindle Hill in Wolcott, where Seth Thomas roamed as a boy and later learned his trade; Break Neck Hill in Middlebury, where Rochambeau's troops rested and foraged during the time of the American Revolution; and Bunker Hill in Waterbury, where nearly 200 years ago the Grilley Brothers began making buttons, creating the first gleaming trickle in what would soon become a manufacturing torrent.

But the rising sun catches more than glimpses of the past in these green hills. It also hits and holds the drumbeat of the present, the hustle and bustle of a region that itself has recently emerged from a long and troubling night into a promising new era.

The new era lives this morning in a thousand ways that reflect the region's diversity: in the busy hum of the interstate as it cuts through West Side Hill in Waterbury, and in the quiet of Bishop's Farm in Cheshire, where apple and pear trees bend toward the light; in the corporate stirrings atop Bullet Hill in Southbury, where IBM's splendid new facility houses 2,500 computer, accounting, and personnel employees, and in the less complicated stirrings of the region's many bakers of good Italian bread as they load hot loaves into waiting delivery trucks; in the

first bells of the day on Academy Hill in Watertown, where the students at Taft School get ready for breakfast, and in the first bell of the day at Peter Paul Company in Naugatuck, where thousands of Mounds candy bars will roll off the line during the next 10 hours.

And so a typical day begins in Greater Waterbury. As 7 A.M. approaches, the region's pulse continues to quicken. In Waterbury itself, the 6:58 train for Grand Central Terminal in New York City begins moving down the line toward the lower Naugatuck Valley. Commuter traffic moves along the highways—I-84 east and west, and Route 8 north and south—into Waterbury or out to New Haven, Hartford, or Upper Fairfield County. The region's highly skilled and celebrated work force checks into hundreds of various manufacturing plants and begins expertly churning out everything from lipstick tubes to imaging scanners, from brass buttons to modems, and from auto parts to photoresists. Likewise, the region's distributors go to work, capitalizing on the relatively uncrowded roads and the nearness to much of the American Northeast to distribute an astonishing range of items, including bottled water, bananas, salt and pepper shakers, the contents of Bloomingdale's catalogue, seafood, and more.

Soon, all is in the light of a new day—and the many advantages of life in Greater Waterbury are revealed.

There is, first of all, the strength inherent in its reputation as a part of the essential Connecticut—a place where Yankee ingenuity and ambition built factories that were the backbone and muscle of industrial America, and the envy of the world. And where hard work and ambition

can *still* be rewarded today.

There is the uncommon industry of its people, their reliability as a work force and their skill as craftsmen.

There is the convenience of its great roads and its proximity to all of Connecticut—to the country charms of Litchfield County and the rest of New England, and to the urban allure of New York and Boston.

And there is the stability of its style of life, with its emphasis on traditional values and strong neighborhood bonds, and its low cost and availability of housing, real estate, and office space in relation to most other parts of Connecticut and certainly to the New York Metropolitan Area. Waterbury has come a long way in recent years, and much of the 13-town region has prospered as well. This process began first with a gratifying burst of self-discovery among the residents themselves, and then with the gradual discovery among outsiders that Waterbury contained most of the advantages of life in Connecticut with relatively few of the disadvantages. And now, new people continue to discover Waterbury every day.

As the region is, in a sense, reborn, the time has come to tell its story once again. But to tell the story of Waterbury properly we must start at the beginning, for it is in the beginning, as the earliest settlers made their way through the wilderness from Farmington, that the great strengths of its people were first revealed.

A bright blue sky and an intense fall foliage create a perfect autumn portrait. Photo by Jack McConnell

A Region Reborn

From Mattatuck Onward

It is a pity that the beautiful old Indian name, Mattatuck, was not retained. But our Puritan ancestors regarded these native words as heathenish, and were in haste to discard and forget them. HENRY BRONSON

It looked like a good home right from the beginning.

As the first white settlers made their winding way down the western slope of Southington Mountain in the spring of 1674, they came upon a peaceful, narrow valley set down amidst a disorderly procession of hills. Some of the hills were brown and oddly treeless, but most of them were thick with chestnut, white pine, sugar maple, oak, and elm. Along the two main rivers, later called Naugatuck and Mad, alluvial deposits had formed natural meadows that showed some promise for agriculture.

The two rivers were the major watercourses, but there was also a whole companion network of streams, ponds, and other wetlands. In general, the water flowed down from the wild higher ground that trailed off into the distance to the north and west. This ample supply of water not only attracted the settlers and eventually secured the future of the place (and its name), but it also provided sustenance to bears, deer, wolves, geese, ducks, and a tremendous profusion of smaller game and freshwater fish.

The natural character of the land had of course not been altered by the aborigines. The Indians did not have a village at what they called *Mattatuck* ("place without trees"), but rather they enjoyed temporary encampments throughout the region—on a promising river bank, a commanding bluff, or near a dependable spring—according to the dictates of the season or the needs of the moment.

This part of the valley, in fact, evidently fell between the juris-

dictions of several tribes of the Algonkian Federation: the Tunxis to the north and the Paugasetts and Quinnipiacs to the south. Despite its many pleasant features, none of the tribes seemed to value the area very highly; indeed as Waterbury historian Dr. Joseph Anderson later pointed out rather sourly: "Historians have hitherto accorded to the territory no charms beyond those known to the hunter; it has been thought that even the Indians held the region in avoidance."

THE PUSH TO SETTLE

But it looked just fine to the settlers, who were from nearby Farmington and who yearned for a place of their own. A year earlier, in 1673, they had petitioned the General Court in Hartford to send out a committee to view the new territory and report back on its suitability as an area for settlement. "We who were sent to view Matitacoocke in reference to plantation, do judge it capable of the same," the committee concluded. Their optimism was not boundless, however. They added their opinion that the area probably could not support any more than 30 families.

Thus encouraged, the 26 founding families of Waterbury left the relative ease and civility of the Farmington River Valley and headed west into the unknown. They traveled single-file along Indian paths, moving up and down the hills and ridges like a determined line of ants negotiating the folds of a picnic blanket. They made it up the steep eastern face of Metacomet Ridge and then gradually dropped down (roughly along the I-84 of today) until they reached the banks of what they would learn to call the Naugatuck River.

We do not know much about those first settlers as they stood there 315 years ago, scanning the hills and fields for suitable homesites. We know the names of the 26 men who signed the petition to the General Court, but there was no great chronicler or journal keeper among them. We can presume that they were, by and large, young men, most with families. And we know through their subse-

ABOVE: The banks of the Farmington River have long been lush and fertile. Photo by Jack McConnell

RIGHT: The Old Township of Waterbury, with nearby villages and rivers, is clearly defined by this map. Courtesy, Mattatuck Museum

PAGES 12-13: A fog enshrouded Connecticut River runs still in the early morning hours. Photo by Jack McConnell

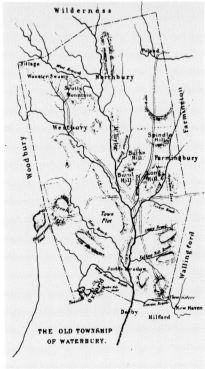

THE OLD TOWNSHIP
OF WATERBURY.

quent actions that their commitment to their new home and to their new lives was fierce.

The group chose, for their first settlement, to cross the river and go up the hill to an area still known today as Town Plot. There they parceled out 8-acre lots and each family agreed to build "a good and fashionable dwelling house 18x16, and 9 feet between joints with a good chimney."

Before any of those houses was completed, however, an Indian war first made its indelible impression upon Waterbury (as all wars would). The brutal King Philip's War forced white settlers throughout southern New England to retreat from the frontiers in order to seek safety and survival in numbers. The settlers, who were probably living and sleeping under temporary shelters, quickly left Town Plot and hurried back to Farmington. But by the spring of 1677, the hostilities had abated and the settlers returned, this time permanently.

Curiously, however, they did not go back to Town Plot. Perhaps for reasons of protection, they decided instead to situate their homes and stake their hopes for the future around a frog-filled bog— which later would become known as the Waterbury Green. This time, they drew out 36 plots of two acres each, with much common grazing and planting land beyond. In September 1677 they closed a land deal with the Tunxis Indians. For an allotment of coats, meat, bread, coin, beer, and cider worth some £38, they bought a piece of land about 16 miles long and 8 miles wide, roughly from southernmost Naugatuck to northernmost Thomaston and encompassing some 130 square miles—in essence what is today known as Greater Waterbury.

And so the people of Mattatuck began at last to settle down, "God-fearing, God-worshiping, God-loved, and we hope, God-loving," according to one historian. But definitely not Indian-loving, he might have added.

The threat to the settlement from Indians was present into the eighteenth century. While relations with the local tribes were friendly (if rather one-sided in outcome), the aggressive Mohawks to the west were not beyond sending raiders into unprotected villages. Throughout the region, particularly between 1689 and 1713, "Crops were destroyed by hostile savages, cattle were driven away, dwellings were burned, men and women were murdered or carried captive . . . the settlements were kept in a state of alarm." Consequently, the new dwellings around the Green remained stockaded for some 35 years, while scouts roamed the woods, sentinels manned strategic outposts, and the men working the fields along the river plain kept their firearms handy.

The settlers were eager to distance themselves from the Indians in other ways as well, most notably by incorporating themselves as the "Town of Waterbury" in 1686. "It is a pity that the beautiful old Indian name, Mattatuck, was not retained," wrote Henry Bronson. "But our Puritan ancestors regarded these native words as heathenish, and were in haste to discard and forget them."

AN IDENTITY IS FORGED

By whatever name, the new settlement did not provide an easy life for its inhabitants. The soil was not everything the farmers had hoped. It was boggy and prone to flooding in some places, while in many others it was rocky and unsuitable for anything but meager grazing. Further, the settlement of homes around the damp, insect-plagued Green likely led to a number of general illnesses.

The settlers, as one of their number wrote in 1689, "living remotely in a corner of the wilderness, brought low by many losses and by much sickness during the space of four years," were about to take two additional major blows. The first was an enormous flood in 1691, in which "their precious meadows, on which they chiefly depended for the support of life, were torn up by the roots and carried away." The second calamity was a "great sickness" that struck in 1712 and lingered in Waterbury for over a year, disabling many

Both Indians and early settlers forged trails through forests of white birch and other vegetation indigenous to the Waterbury region, much like the forest seen in this photograph by Georgia Sheron

and killing a full 10 percent of the residents.

But the Waterburians, as would always be the case, were not easily put off by adversity. They hung on, they made do, and, quite unknowingly, they began to hammer out a personality for the city to come. They had not chosen an easy place in which to live, but it was their place. If the land wouldn't provide for them, then they would provide for themselves.

Even so, Waterbury did little more than eke out an existence during most of the 1700s. The farmers were too busy scratching out a living to have much time for anything else. Some early signs of initiative did exist, however, including establishment of a grain mill on the Mad River in 1680, a saw mill in 1682, and a fulling mill on Great Brook (now an underground watercourse) in 1692. The earliest glimmerings of a manufacturing future could be read in the production in 1705 of oaken staves for export to the "wine islands in the West Indies."

Gradually, a rough sort of civilization came to the new town. A

Precious meadows such as this one supported the lifeblood of the early settlers. Courtesy, Waterbury Convention and Visitors Commission

The First Congregational Church, seen here, was photographed in 1895. Courtesy, Mattatuck Museum

schoolhouse and a meetinghouse were in place by the 1720s, while the Naugatuck River was first bridged at about the same time. Waterbury gradually became something of a crossroads as horse paths were hacked out to Woodbury (whose fertile Pomperaug Valley had first drawn settlers in 1673), to Farmington and Hartford, to Meriden, and to New Haven. Churches were established as well, first the Congregational in 1691, then the Episcopalian in 1740 (much later came the Baptist church in 1803, the Methodist in 1815, and the Catholic in 1847). Indeed, by all indications, including a modest but steady growth in population, as the 1700s progressed so did Waterbury—even though the progress may not always have been visible to outsiders.

"At last we got to Waterbury," wrote Bethia Baldwin in a 1770 diary entry as she traveled from her home in Norwich to Danbury. "There we put up. Oh, law! Horrible. Nasty. Drinkt some flip. Could eat no supper. Went to bed. Oh, bless me, what nasty sheets . . ."

Ten years later one of the Marquis de Lafayette's aides, traveling with the French general through Waterbury, remarked only: "The village is frightful and without resources."

What those observers did not notice—and what their haughty ranks would repeatedly miss in the years ahead—was that there was (and is) much more to Waterbury, and the entire region, than meets the eye. In the late eighteenth century, for instance, they did not see, or hear, or feel the great change that was afoot. The sleepy town was waking up at last to a new age of ingenuity and industry.

Located on West Main Street, the Second Congregational Church is depicted circa 1895. Courtesy, Mattatuck Museum

The "Great Transition," as it would later be called, was going to work in the hearts and minds and in the workshops of the people along the Naugatuck.

As the Revolutionary War drew to a close, a great sense of freedom and restless ambition was sweeping across the new nation. Everywhere in America, entrepreneurs and visionaries, inventors and peddlers, were free to test their products and their ideas before a new and eager market. It was the moment that Waterbury had been waiting for. As quickly as it could, it cast off its agricultural disguise, rolled up its sleeves, and began making things.

MANUFACTURING BEGINS

As the century drew to a close, Timothy Dwight, the president of Yale, visited Waterbury during his travels through New England. "Waterbury is a pleasant town, built chiefly on a single street," he wrote. But Dwight also took a closer look that revealed the first fitful breezes of the manufacturing storm: "Several manufactures have been carried on in this town with spirit and success, particularly that of clocks," Dwight wrote.

Lucien Bisbee published this detail of "Waterbury from West Side Hill" in 1837. Courtesy, Mattatuck Museum

These are considered as keeping time with nearly as much regularity as those which are made of the customary materials [Waterbury's were made of wood]. They also last long; and being sold at a very moderate price, are spread over a prodigious extent of country, to the great convenience of a vast number of people, who would otherwise have no means of regulating their various businesses. Gilt buttons have also been made here in considerable quantities; not inferior in strength and beauty to those which are imported.

Indeed, Waterbury's great manufacturing heritage was born in but-

tons and wooden clocks. Button making had begun as early as 1750, really as a backyard industry, as Joseph Hopkins produced the silver and silver-plated variety. By 1790, the Grilley Brothers in Bunker Hill were making pewter buttons that were in turn sold throughout the new nation by an aggressive corps of itinerant peddlers.

In 1802 the big move came when the Grilleys joined with Abel and Levi Porter to begin the manufacture of brass buttons alongside the Mad River. This was the beginning of what one day would become the Scovill Manufacturing Company, and it also marked the beginning of Waterbury's long and spectacular association with brass.

The manufacture of wooden clocks began around 1790 by James Harrison, who was the first local manufacturer to introduce waterpower to his task in 1800. Nearby, in what would later be known as Terryville, Eli Terry began his clock company in 1795, selling out to Seth Thomas 15 years later. In that same year, 1810, three men went into business making wooden clocks on Great Brook in Waterbury near the corner of North Main and Cherry streets, a concern that would eventually grow into the Waterbury Clock Company, and, much later, Timex.

A regional gazetteer published in 1819 could still say of Waterbury: "In this, like the other towns in the county, agriculture is the principal business of the inhabitants." But it could also remark that "the late war [War of 1812] had a favorable influence in stimulating the naturally enterprising spirit of its citizens."

Indeed, Waterbury took to manufacturing with complete enthusiasm. It is regularly pointed out in chronicles of the city that there was no natural reason for it to become an industrial center; it was not near a source of raw materials, it was not situated on a port or even on a navigable river. From this distant vantage point, it almost seems as if Waterburians *willed* their own success. Certainly, they

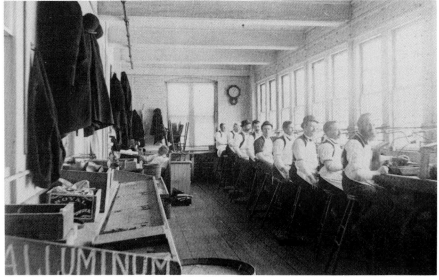

Inside the Scovill Manufacturing Company, these men worked long hours, as depicted in this 1891 photo taken in the burnishing room. Courtesy, Mattatuck Museum

ABOVE: Eli Terry began producing clocks in 1795. Courtesy, Mattatuck Museum

ABOVE RIGHT: Seth Thomas purchased the clock company that Eli Terry had begun 15 years earlier. Courtesy, Mattatuck Museum

took advantage of every opportunity and went far beyond the normal course of business in order to succeed.

For example, the traditional center of the brass industry existed in England. When the War of 1812 created a period in which no exports from England were allowed, the Waterburians took advantage. They began rolling their own brass for their buttons, a technique taken up by Aaron Benedict and the Benedict and Burnham Manufacturing Company, which in later years, in combination with other local brass concerns, would become the American Brass Company.

But the Waterburians did not stop there. In 1817 Abel Porter and Company, later to become Scovill, scored a huge coup when it spirited an expert brass craftsman named James Croft away from his factory in England and brought him to Waterbury so he could reveal to the eager Yanks a few trade secrets. It is even said that one Waterburian, Israel Holmes, ran an excellent trade by smuggling skilled English metalworkers and toolmakers in casks out of England (where the government was trying to prevent the loss of skilled craftsmen) and through the Port of New York.

And so by such unusual ambition did Waterbury continue to roll along. Its population in 1820 had been around 3,500; by 1850, it was 5,137; and, according to the U.S. census, by 1900, Waterbury had mushroomed into a city of 51,139 souls.

Workers from the American Brass Company at Ansonia posed for this photo in 1899. Courtesy, Mattatuck Museum

PRODUCING FOR THE WORLD

As the factories grew, especially after 1850, and the call went out for workers, men and women seemingly from all over Europe responded. The first to arrive were the Irish, a fellow named Cornelius Donnelly having been spotted (like a windblown sea bird) on a downtown street as early as 1832. Joseph Anderson described the early Irish arrivals, but he could have been referring to any of the waves of hopeful immigrants when he wrote:

They were the proverbial 'handful,' but strong of faith, robust of physique, self-reliant, and confident that the future held much in reserve. They came to stay, to cast their lot with their fellows . . . and to assist, as far as they could, in laying deep and strong the foundations of what is now a flourishing city.

They came from Ireland and from Germany, from French Can-

In 1850 Jared Thompson painted this image of the Waterbury Green. Courtesy, Mattatuck Museum

ada and Sweden, from Lithuania, Russia, from the southern United States, and eventually in the greatest number, from Italy. Basically, they came to work in the shops, to become, in the eventual Waterbury vernacular, "shop rats." They went to the casting shops, the clock shops, the rolling mills, and wherever else they were offered steady work and a decent wage. And often, as they set about making their new homes and raising their families, the very hard work and the difficulties of life in a new place made them think wistfully of their homelands, as this stanza from "Scovill's Rolling Mill" by Michael "Faker" Sullivan illustrates:

You may go down to New York, my boy,
and hear the ocean roar,
You imagine you see mother standing
at the cabin door,
Crying, 'Darling Jack, come back again
and the old farm you can till,'
Then no more you'll roam from your
native home to work in the Rolling Mill.

But for the most part, the new citizens of Waterbury looked forward rather than behind them. They established churches and social halls. They brought music and sports, new foods, and cultural traditions with them and tossed them into the melting pot. With alarming speed, Waterbury was transformed from the sleepy farm town of 1820 to the vibrant, ethnically diverse city of the post-Civil War period.

And the factories boomed. On February 9, 1846, Waterbury Brass Company rolled its first brass in what was the largest brass mill in America. In 1850, the Scovill Manufacturing Company officially came into being on the site of Abel Porter's old one-horse mill. New factories seemed to open up every other week, most notably Waterbury Farrel Foundry; Holmes, Booth, & Hayden; American Pin Company; Rogers and Hamilton; Waterbury Buckle; Steele and Johnson; Waterbury Manufacturing Company; and the Waterbury Button Company.

By 1873 James M. Baily, a visitor from Danbury, could say,

Waterbury is prolific with manufacturers. The modern woman receives from here many of the artificial adornments that go to make her a source of constant attraction and alarm to the contemplative masculine. Waterbury has twelve or thirteen thousand inhabitants—all busy—the finest library in the state, a handsome

This Anaconda-American Brass Company plant was the former Benedict and Burnham Manufacturing Company building. Courtesy, Mattatuck Museum

ABOVE: These brass buttons are currently on display at the Waterbury Companies Inc. Photo by Robert Houser

FACING PAGE: Commemorating the Civil War, this monument is located at the west end of the green in front of the Mattatuck Museum. Photo by Georgia Sheron

city hall, three railroads, a daily paper, and a hot, tedious walk from the depot to the business centre.

In the 20 or so years following the Civil War, Waterbury and the world of manufacturing in general entered an era of almost romantic intensity. The Waterbury Watch Company, for instance—the producer of good, cheap, mass-produced watches—was pouring out some 1,000 watches a day in the 1880s, a shiny stream that drew Waterburian S.W. Kellogg near: "If you will ride through the streets of Waterbury in the evening," he wrote, "you will see no more beautiful sight than the Waterbury watch factory, all lit up as it is from turret to foundation stone, like a blazing palace of light for the cunning workmanship that is going on within its walls."

Historian William J. Pape wrote of the period around the turn of the century:

It was literally true and had been for years that it was almost impossible to make anything from an umbrella to a pair of shoes or a suit of clothes, from a small electric motor to a locomotive or a battleship, from a trunk or handbag to a great office building or

Advertisements like this one from the Waterbury Watch Company, circa 1885, were abundant and well-recognized. Courtesy, Mattatuck Museum

"The Waterbury."

A WELL-WATCHED GIRL WITH A TICK-LISH TIME OF IT

This Young Lady, like every Sensible Young Lady, has supplied herself with a

Waterbury Watch.

The Most Perfect, Genuine Time-Piece for the Least Amount of Money.

A STEM WINDER.

LARGE, CLEAR DIAL.

ACCURATE TIME.

A Watch complete in every sense, manufactured in large numbers and all superfluous machinery discarded, so as to bring it in price within the reach of everyone.

Can be Repaired at any Time at the Factory at a cost not exceeding Fifty Cents.

Every Watch Tested before It Leaves the Factory and Every Watch Guaranteed.

THE WATERBURY WATCH COMPANY,

GEORGE MERRITT, Selling Agent.

52 Maiden Lane, New York City.   Factory, Waterbury, Conn.

*hotel, without creating a demand for something made of brass or
copper and sending to Waterbury for it.*

A partial inventory, taken in 1897, of the manufactured goods
pouring out of Waterbury and into the world at large reveals a
fascinating and bedazzling array: oil burners, lamps, clocks and
watches; plain and elastic webbing, buckles and garters; upholstery
nails, drawer pulls, hinges; dress pins, safety pins, and buttons (ivory,
cloth, and brass); bicycle pumps, valves, name plates, cyclometers,
spoke nipples, chains, pedals, and other parts; rivets and burs, eyelets; ornaments for the millinary trade, for bookbinders, for makers
of fancy leather goods; every variety of metallic trimming, powder
flasks, fulminate caps, steel traps and cow bells; house boilers and
plumber's fittings, harness trimmings; machinery for working sheet
metal and wire into every possible shape, form and condition,
ranging from the heaviest rolling mills work down to delicate
machines for minute screws and tiny articles of wire; sash, doors
and blinds; sand-cast articles in brass and German silver; parts for
incandescent lights; paper boxes, perfumery, silverware, stationery,
drugs, and toilet articles.

Thus engaged, Waterbury was ready to enter its great Golden
Age. As the century drew to a close, it was a growing, confident
place. Its hard-working population was spreading out from the
center of town, onto the many surrounding hills, and into the
surrounding towns. Indeed, by 1900 all the towns in the Greater
Waterbury area had been well established. Parts of the original
130-square-mile Waterbury had been taken to establish, or help
create, Watertown in 1780; Middlebury in 1790; Wolcott in 1796;
Prospect in 1827; and Naugatuck in 1844. In addition, Cheshire had
been incorporated out of Wallingford in 1780; both Bethlehem and
Southbury were established in 1787 (each formerly a part of Woodbury); Oxford was incorporated in 1798, Beacon Falls in 1871, and
Thomaston in 1875.

The region had become an entity of sorts, but each town established a distinct and fiercely protected local personality. Most of the
towns remained largely agricultural in 1900, although Naugatuck and
Thomaston were notable exceptions.

And in the center of it all sat Waterbury, the increasingly prosperous and self-confident hub. The city had become a transportation
center and a regional commercial center. For its time, it was a city
of the highest technical know-how and skill. By many of the usual mea-
surements, Waterbury had become a leading American city. There
was no reason for the people living there to believe that the future
was not one of limitless growth and prosperity. And for many years,
for a whole half-century in fact, they would be correct.

Decline and Rebirth

> *The same things that made Waterbury a great city in the first place were still there. We just had to put them to work.* JOHN ERRICHETTI

Despite the present resurgence in its fortunes, Waterbury probably has never experienced a more acute outburst of civic pride and self-congratulations than it did during its Old Home Celebration on November 25, 26, and 27 in 1915.

It was during that three-day period that the city finally paused in its 100 years of hard work so it could officially recognize its own ascendance, its very good fortune, and the fruits of its labor. "It is securely alleged that Waterbury is the center of the world's brass industry," proclaimed the *Official Souvenir Programme,* and, indeed, the three-day gala was a celebration of that lofty status. Waterbury had arrived, and this was the coming-out party.

There was a carnival and fireworks and a parade each day. There was a Governor's Dinner and a Governor's Ball. There were dedications of the new flagpole on the Green, the new clock on the Green, and the new city hall. The previous city hall had been destroyed by arson in 1912, a crime referred to at some length in the *Programme:* "The last chapter in the now famous million-dollar adventure of Bernard C. Murray, the fire-bug, is written in the dedication of Waterbury's beautiful new City Hall," the account read. "When Murray, whose fiery passion is now slowly wasting itself under the restraining hands of the Matteawan authorities, started the first of 13 incendiary fires," he little could have realized what was to grow up out of his misdeeds.

The writer then went on to breathlessly describe the new building, with its "blushing red" brick, its "chaste and snowlike encasements," its chandeliers "swinging happily," and its "modest timepiece that chimes so gladly the hour of the day."

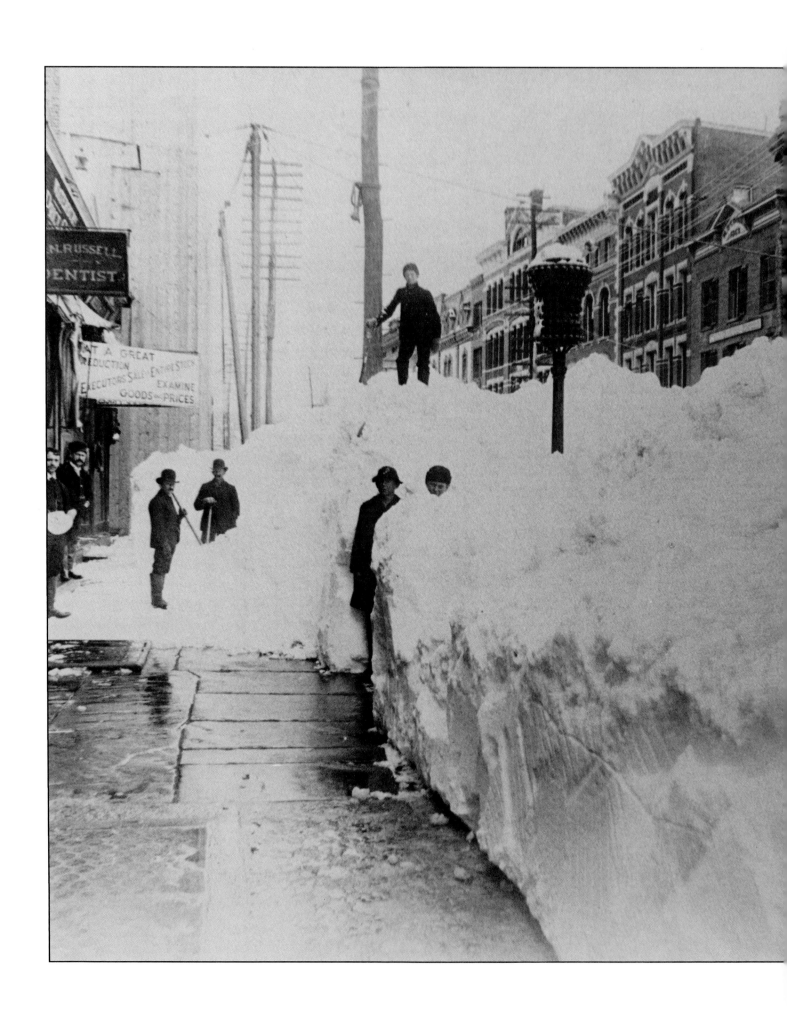

"PINS BY THE BILLIONS"

The city, it seems, was in a state of euphoria, but it was a euphoria that was clearly justified by events. Waterbury's economy had never been so healthy. Even before the outbreak of World War I, the factories were prospering. Now, with a war on in Europe, they were bursting at the seams.

"It has been remarked for years," wrote historian William J. Pape during that soaring period,

that wherever a man may travel, he will find metal goods that have come from Waterbury. The sun, literally, never sets upon the work of Waterbury's hands. This draws to her the inventor, the skilled mechanic and the merchant from all parts of the nation, and from distant lands. They come here to develop their ideas, to gain their industrial training, to supervise the manufacture of their wares. Sooner or later, everybody who has a small article which can be made out of the metals in which we are skilled in working, turns up in Waterbury to ask our price for making his goods, or our help in devising cunning machinery that will turn them out for him. There is perpetual circulation between Waterbury and the

PAGES 30-31: Construction on the present Waterbury City Hall, designed by Cass Gilbert, was completed in 1915. Photo by Barry Rabinowitz

FACING PAGE: Following this circa 1898 blizzard, many Waterburians were required to shovel snow for long hours. Courtesy, Mattatuck Museum

BELOW: The fifth annual banquet of the Beacon Falls Rubber Shoe Company was held in the ballroom of the Elton Hotel in 1915. Courtesy, Mattatuck Museum

markets of all the world, from which the community perhaps gains as much or more than it imparts, so that at the present time the city and her sister communities up and down the valley are known as reservoirs of mechanics and machinists of the highest training, intelligence and inventive skill.

Tens of thousands of men and women were at work in the region's brass mills and in the various attendant industries. In a situation that often accompanies good economic times, there existed in

All the citizens of Waterbury turned out for the annual Blakeslee sleigh ride, circa 1900. Courtesy, Mattatuck Museum

In 1899 workers pose amid the machinery inside this shoe hardware department. Courtesy, Mattatuck Museum

the Waterbury area both a labor shortage and a housing shortage. Such was the might of the large mills in 1915, however, that in some cases they supplied their own housing to their workers. American Brass, Chase Metal Works, the Waterbury Tool Company, and the Oakville Company were among the companies that built affordable housing for their laborers. It was in 1915 that Scovill built 150 brick houses and offered them for sale to employees for $4,200 to $4,700 on a monthly installment plan. Scovill also constructed barracks for male workers who had come in from out of town, out of state, or even out of the country, charging them 50 cents a week for a bed and a shower.

But Scovill could well afford such largess. During World War I it was to manufacture some 2 billion brass cups for cartridge shells, 443 million bullet jackets, 21 million time fuses for shrapnel, and 19 million 75mm shell cases, just to name a few items. The situation at the other factories was similar. The war in Europe may have had its detractors—and many young city men lost their lives in it—but Waterbury in general was not a place to protest a call to arms, not as long as it was Waterbury that was supplying the arms.

Located on the green, the Elton Hotel was completed in 1905. Courtesy, Mattatuck Museum

The prosperity was spreading throughout the region as well. While certain of the area towns, such as Woodbury, Southbury, Bethlehem, Oxford, Cheshire, Prospect, Wolcott, and Watertown remained quiet farm towns, the cities in the valley were busy following Waterbury's lead. Indeed, as someone described the Naugatuck Valley at the time: "There is hardly in the world such a narrow compass of territory in which there is such an intensity of production and such a genius for industrial leadership."

Naugatuck in 1915 was described as a "thriving manufacturing city" with a population of around 15,000 and some 66 buildings devoted to milling and manufacturing. Naugatuck, of course, had become home of the rubber industry, largely through the pioneering efforts of Charles Goodyear, and it busied itself in churning out some 60,000 pairs of rubber boots and shoes every day.

Beacon Falls, although still a very small town, had become home to the Beacon Falls Rubber Shoe Company and was a major purveyor of powder flasks and whip sockets. The company itself was

rather remarkable, having built a theater and a dance hall in town for its workers, and maintained a company band that every noon played selections out in front of the plant.

Thomaston was also described as "an industrial community" with a population of around 4,000 in 1915. It was home to the Seth Thomas Clock Company, and had been since 1812 when Seth Thomas broke away from his partnership in Plymouth to seek his fortune west of the Naugatuck River.

The prosperity in the region was unprecedented, but so was the wisdom and style with which its citizens responded to their growth. Those who gathered on November 26, 1915, in front of the new city hall on Grand Street in Waterbury, for example, could take pride in that splendid new temple to local government, but there was also much else—especially new buildings—of which to be proud.

The first wave of twentieth century construction in Waterbury had come following the great fire of 1902 in which 21 downtown build-

Waterbury Hospital was constructed in 1911. Courtesy, Mattatuck Museum

ings were destroyed and 18 damaged. As a result many of the fine commercial buildings that still line Bank Street and Grand Street date from 1903. Of other buildings still well-recognized in the city today, the Elton Hotel on the Green went up in 1905, St. Mary's Hospital and the railroad station in 1909, Waterbury Hospital, the Kendrick Street courthouse, and the Masonic Temple (now home to the Mattatuck Museum) all in 1911, the Lilley Building on the Green in 1912, and the American Brass Company headquarters, curving around lower Grand Street, in 1913.

The completion of City Hall in 1915 was to set off another spate of construction of superb buildings, including several by the respected architect Cass Gilbert. Of Gilbert's Waterbury buildings, five (including City Hall, Chase Building, and Citytrust Building) survive side by side along Grand and Field streets.

In addition, those citizens parading through the streets in the autumn of 1915 could take pride in the city's wonderful new Hamilton Park, which was first laid out in 1901 but which did not really come into its own until the summer of 1913, when "the entire population seemed to regard it as a playground." (That population would also have been happy to know that the first sketchy renderings of the future Fulton Park were in 1915 being inked out on city drawing boards.)

As compared to today, this image of the green and Exchange Place appears quite sedate. Courtesy, Mattatuck Museum

Waterburians could be proud, too, of the 25 manufacturing buildings worth some $50 million that had been erected since 1900, of the very rapidly improving street, sewer, and water systems, and of the city's newfound status as a major rail center (86 passenger trains moved in and out of the vast new depot every day, and, in New England, only Boston moved more freight).

Further, with the recent establishment of the Waterbury Chamber of Commerce, the city's story was now getting out to the world. "Waterbury has something on everyone," was the Chamber's cry, or, more specifically, the cry of Charles A. Colley, the organization's energetic president.

"Prior to the inception of the Chamber of Commerce," someone wrote in 1915, "Waterbury plodded peacefully along, indifferent to the glitter of world-wide recognition. But with Mr. C.A.C. as its president, the dormant flame of traditional pride, plentifully fed with the stimulating effects of Mr. Colley's enthusiasm, hysterically worked itself into a contagious blaze."

And the greatest portion of the local pride remained in brass. It was in the city's motto: *Quid Aere Perennius* (What is so lasting as brass?). It was in the very fiber of the daily life of the city, at least

ABOVE: Goodyear's Vulcanite Court, featuring various rubber products, is illustrated here. Courtesy, Mattatuck Museum

BELOW: J. Schlegel's Billiard Parlor attracted only the finest customers. Courtesy, Mattatuck Museum

according to one visitor, who commented: "Brass is the life of Waterbury; but for it the city would be no city . . . You hear it, smell it,
see it, feel it everywhere."

And, during the great celebration of 1915, the association of Waterbury and brass caused at least one local poet to burst forth in enthusi-
astic verse:

Pins by the billions,
Both safety and plain,
Our watches by millions
Gave the dollar a name!*

Buttons and buckles,
Match boxes and lamps,
Even brass knuckles,
Hair pins and clamps.
Eyelets, shoe hardware,
Rings, hooks, and eyes,
Trinkets you all wear,
Medals you prize.

Brass the foundation
Of all ornaments,
Blanks for a nation—
Your nickels and cents.

Steels for the corset
(Ne'er known to break),
Lest you forget,
Are of Brass City make.

And if it's now true
Nothing on you we sight,
It's a Brass City screw
Holds the coffin lid tight.

In about 1930, Sunnyside Avenue was the location of this Lithuanian market. Courtesy, Mattatuck Museum

(*This reference is to a famous cheap Waterbury watch of the nineteenth century: "The watch that made the dollar famous.")

From November 1915, the future seemed exceedingly bright.
No one parading happily through the city streets would have guessed
that the nails in Waterbury's economic coffin were also made of brass.

ADAPTING TO CHANGE

The good times lasted for decades to come, but the seeds of change
were planted along the way and their fruition was inevitable. In

1922 Waterbury's American Brass merged with Anaconda Copper Mining Company. In 1929, Chase Brass merged with Kennecott Copper. These new conglomerates would not remain as loyal to Waterbury as the local owners had been, or, as one brass worker would later point out: "We didn't realize that the bigger corporations could unload a particular plant without any feelings, where the Chase family did everything possible to maintain the operation."

By the late 1930s technological advances began to accelerate the loss of jobs. A new breed of employee known as the industrial engineer began to show up at the big plants, where he introduced to bewildered workers the concept of efficiency. As one worker put it: "We had eight men . . . one of these hatchet men, he come in, he studied it and studied it and finally they eliminated it down to three men. He'd come out and just sit there for months and study how he could eliminate men. He'd check it and check it and finally they'd eliminate a man."

Cooking up a storm in the late 1800s, the Young Women's Friendly League held this cooking class to share their favorite recipes. Courtesy, Mattatuck Museum

During World War II, this young woman removes machine castings from the furnace at the Chase Company. Courtesy, Mattatuck Museum

The inevitable was granted a reprieve of sorts by the outbreak of World War II and, again, the need for the enormous amount of war supplies that only places like Waterbury were equipped to supply. One wartime observer noted that, "Situated in some of the most interesting countryside in New England, the valleys of the Naugatuck and Mad rivers, and set on the slopes of the somewhat precipitous brown hills that rise from the rivers, Waterbury presents a picture of that industrial America which bodes ill for the Axis."

Bode ill it did, but when the war ended, a 30-year period of decline set in. In the big plants, automation reduced the number of jobs, especially at entry levels. In addition, the brass industry itself declined, its many products finally giving way to plastics and aluminum. The company owners, who were often not local persons with local concerns, reinvested their profits elsewhere. The plants began to run down and the city began to suffer.

Those looking for a symbolic and especially bruising end to Waterbury's great industrial era often point to the Flood of 1955. A tremendous rain on August 18 and 19 of that year fell on already sodden ground throughout Connecticut. The result in the Naugatuck Valley was disastrous. As the great torrent hurtled down from the north it broke through dams, took out bridges, tore up roads and railroad

tracks, and swept through houses and factories. Eighty-seven persons died in the valley, including 24 in Waterbury. One hundred and thirty-seven companies were destroyed or greatly damaged. And when the floodwaters finally receded, it seemed as if something in the fighting spirit of a great city had been swept away as well.

During the next two decades, Waterbury rocked on its heels. The Vietnam War kept the factories going to some degree, but it wasn't nearly enough. By the 1970s the downtown streets appeared shuttered and dark. Property values stagnated. New building came to a standstill. Waterbury had an especially bad year in 1976, as Scovill

Following the flood of 1955, a pile of debris lodges against the West Main Street bridge. Courtesy, Mattatuck Museum

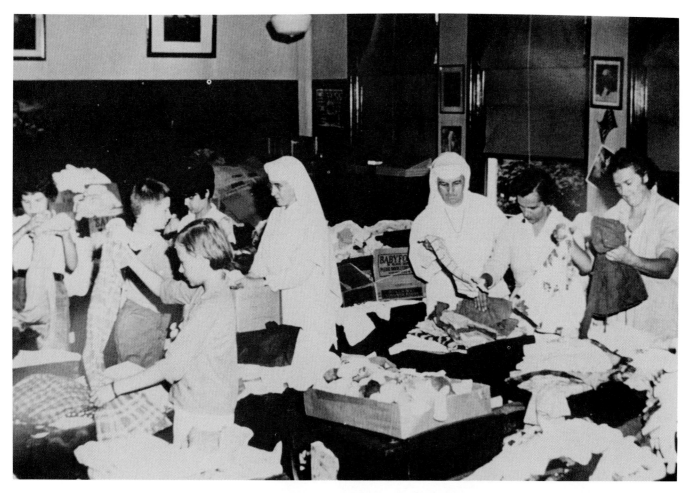

ABOVE: On August 24 the Sisters of St. Joseph's School helped to distribute clothing to the needy following the flood of 1955. Courtesy, Mattatuck Museum

RIGHT: Inside the Coca-Cola Bottling Company, citizens line up for the distribution of drinking water following the flood of 1955. Courtesy, Mattatuck Museum

sold its brass operations, Chase Brass closed up shop, and the city's un-employment rate shot up to 15.5 percent. Four years later Anaconda shut down. Waterbury had reached bottom. Even many of the city's famed public clocks, for so long a source of great local pride, stopped keeping the correct time—and no one seemed to care. Waterburi-ans, most of whom never really thought the day would come, grew bit-ter and fatalistic. Their city had become known as a place to avoid.

But this is a story with a happy ending. Where some observers saw nothing but desolation and loss, others saw opportunity. Where some people went so far as to say that Waterbury was dying, others saw the first glimmerings of a rebirth. If it had been hard work, hard thinking, and willpower that had built Waterbury in the first place, so it would be with the city's renaissance.

"You didn't have to be a genius to see what was going to happen in Waterbury," said Norman Drubner, a local attorney and devel-oper who did not hesitate to act on what he saw. "All you had to do was look at the big picture. You could see the economic wave from New York coming our way, you could see the expansion of the ser-vice economy, and you could see Waterbury, with all its natural attri-butes, sitting right there in the middle of it all. I couldn't understand why people were throwing up their hands and leaving."

ASSETS, ACTION, AND GROWTH

Indeed, in the last 10 years, Waterbury has staged a brilliant come-back. Its economy, no longer subject to the whims of a single indus-try, has grown and diversified. Its institutions have been reinvigorated. Its splendid downtown (preserved in large part thanks to the efforts in the late 1970s of Waterbury Action to Conserve Our Heritage) has been restored and put into new, vigorous use. Most importantly and fundamentally, its citizens have demonstrated a reawakened pride in their city and its fortunes.

The transformation actually began even as the last lights were go-ing out on the brass industry in the late 1970s.

"I agree that the future for Waterbury looked bleak," said devel-oper John Errichetti, whose latest projects include two office build-ings on the Green. "But you had to remember one thing: The same things that made Waterbury a great city in the first place were still there. We just had to put them to work."

First in the city's favor was its location. It was on a major high-way interchange, midway between New York and Boston, and less than 40 minutes from Hartford, Fairfield County, Long Island Sound, and the Litchfield Hills.

Second, the city's infrastructure was sound, even superb. Its wa-ter delivery system was among the best in the nation. Its fire depart-ment was outstanding. Its downtown building stock, virtually

Kendrick Street is the location of the Superior Court building. Photo by Barry Rabinowitz

untouched by the redevelopment bulldozers of the 1960s, was an architectural treasure trove.

Most important were the Waterburians themselves. As always, they made up a work force that was highly skilled, highly motivated, and very stable. They had created a city that was family- and neighborhood-oriented, with comparatively low crime rates and few of the social problems that were crippling other cities of similar size in the Northeast.

It wasn't long before Waterburians realized what they still had, and before others began to realize it too. Companies ranging in size from tiny entrepreneurships to such giants as IBM were quick to seize upon the significance of the Waterbury area's location, its

This Plaza on the Green is a contemporary structure using red brick building materials to better blend with the surrounding older buildings. Photo by Barry Rabinowitz

affordability, and the skills of its workers. Foresighted developers began refurbishing magnificent historic buildings and erecting modern ones in the city's bustling downtown, creating a pleasing blend of old and new. Housing starts multiplied. Commercial establishments, from new restaurants to theaters to retail outlets, opened up and found an interested public.

"When we first opened up the Westside Lobster House, we found that the people in this area had very sophisticated tastes in such things as food and enterainment, but really not that many places to go," said Bob DeZinno, who now runs a network of restaurants in the region. "Waterbury and the whole region have really come into their own in the last ten years."

With the restored pride and the booming economy came also a new interest in heritage and culture. The Mattatuck Museum built a splendid new home on the Waterbury Green, and, at present, the Palace Theatre on East Main Street is undergoing a multimillion- dollar facelift so it again can be home to concerts and theatrical productions.

Waterbury today stands in proud contrast to the city of 10 years ago. It has recognized its fundamental strengths, it has acted upon them, and it has been rewarded with a new era of growth.

"The most remarkable thing about present-day Waterbury—aside from its recovery from near economic death—is the number of opportunities that still exist here," said Howard Plomann, executive director of the city's development agency. "That's probably our strongest point today."

Indeed, Waterbury remains a relatively affordable place in which to live and in which to build or move a business. Homeowners can still find bargains in the city's solid housing stock, while businesses and professionals can find office space in old or new buildings at reasonable rates—and even large companies can learn what has drawn such

Waterbury's U.S. Post Office is yet another architecturally notable building within the city proper. Photo by Barry Rabinowitz

Once a carriage house for the storage of transportation means, the Peck Carriage House has now been renovated, and houses various commercial enterprises. Photo by Barry Rabinowitz

impressive names as IBM to make a home in and around Waterbury.

"This area is really the place to be for those who wish all the benefits of life in Connecticut without the crowding and the extreme prices you find in other parts of the state," said Plomann. "Opportunities still exist here for those who wish to join Waterbury in its new era, and to demonstrate that the old virtues are still the best virtues."

It's likely that the Old Yankees, whose hard work and ingenuity helped make Waterbury in the first place, would be happy to see their city today. They'd be proud to see that the climate they helped to create is still invigorating, the work ethic they helped to inspire is still active, and the city they once called their own is still thriving.

And present-day Waterburians are happy to see it, too.

Old Values, New Economy

> *I think Waterbury's move forward shows what can happen when you retain your basic values . . . and when you are proud of who you are and where you came from.* EUGENE SHUGRUE

The Waterbury region's resurgence—although it may seem sudden to some—has been far from an overnight transformation. It first saw light as a strictly local phenomenon, a quiet self-confidence among residents that the natural attributes of the region—most notably its location—combined with promising economic trends and their own hard work would bring about a long-awaited change for the better.

The rebirth was nurtured within the gradually widening circle of new businesses and interested outsiders—particularly those from more expensive parts of the Northeast—who took a hard look at the Waterbury region and saw nothing but opportunity.

The resurgence is today evidenced in all sorts of activity, from an export-fueled surge in manufacturing and manufacturing jobs, to a regional boom in retail sales, to a long-anticipated run-up in service-sector and white-collar positions, and, finally, to Waterbury's emergence as a last, stubborn bastion of affordable housing.

"This is Waterbury's time, says economist David J. Walker, first vice president of People's Bank in Hartford. According to Walker:

Waterbury and the Naugatuck Valley will find increasing favor with workers and employers as its economic vitality strengthens. Very quietly and very slowly, the region has caught up with the rest of the state. Not only is housing available there, but it's also affordable. Waterbury, overall, is in what I'd call an economic boom; it's the unpolished jewel of Connecticut.

First a few basic facts about this "unpolished jewel" and the 12 towns surrounding it. The region had a population of approximately 250,000 in 1988, up from 237,000 in 1980. According to the 1980 census, the region enjoys a wide ethnic diversity, and racial minorities represent 8 percent of the total population.

In the region the median age is 33, more than half the population 25 and older attended college, and the per capita income is generally in keeping with Connecticut's ranking as the richest state in the nation.

A closer look at a map of the 13-town Greater Waterbury, however, reveals in some detail several of the various elements that have led the region out of the shadows and back into the light of day.

To the north, as a symbol of the region's adaptability and continuing manufacturing strength, stands the huge old Seth Thomas clock factory in Thomaston. Seth Thomas lumbered out of town some years ago, but new and diversified industrial life has sprung up in its wake. Today, the refurbished clock factory houses 16 small businesses busily employing some 300 workers in a variety of trades.

To the east, as a symbol of the region's outstanding retail potential (the area enjoyed more retail sales in 1987 than any other area in the state outside of Fairfield County), lies a large parcel of land near the intersection of routes I-691 and 10 in Cheshire that is ex-

PAGES 50-51: Basic values and economic trends have facilitated the tremendous growth of the Waterbury region. Photo by Barry Rabinowitz

BELOW: Brand new housing projects, such as Ferncliff at Cables, have been affordably priced. Photo by Robert Houser

pected one day to be the home of the Apple Valley Mall. The large mall, only one of several vying for attention in the region (including one in Watertown and one in Waterbury itself), is expected to provide area shoppers with the upscale merchandise they previously had to travel to Stamford or to Farmington to purchase.

To the south, symbolic of the region's exceptional strategic strength, is the Waterbury-Oxford Airport in Oxford. This modern, state-owned facility is a little-known and little-used gem, certainly a key element in Waterbury's untapped potential—and also typical of the region's transportation assets, which include crisscrossing major highways, daily passenger and freight rail service from Waterbury, limousine service to the Hartford and New York airports, and service from five bus lines.

Finally, to the west, symbolic of the region's growth and great potential in non-manufacturing fields, stands IBM's enormous new facility in Southbury. The one-million-square-foot complex, high above Route I-84, houses the company's personnel, accounting, and computer divisions—and a total of some 2,500 workers.

"When you look at a map of Connecticut and you are looking for a region that has excellent roads, a good airport, affordable housing, and room for growth, your eye keeps returning to Waterbury and the Naugatuck Valley," says David Driver, former marketing direc-

From this aerial view, Interstate 84, St. Mary's Hospital, and the White Cross helipad are visible. Photo by Georgia Sheron

Grand Street is the location of a variety of businesses. Photo by Barry Rabinowitz

tor for the state's Department of Economic Development. "Some have known about it for a long time, but others are just learning. The region is really very well situated."

Indeed, just as Waterbury has always teetered right in the middle of Red Sox territory and Yankee territory, it now sits right in between New England's healthy service and manufacturing opportunities and the expansion northward from New York and Fairfield County of corporate headquarters and their many attendant needs. And Waterbury is ready, come what may.

Industrially, it has learned bitterly but well the lessons of diversification. Commercially and professionally, its downtown, with its many refurbished buildings, is among the most attractive in Southern New England. And from a viewpoint of simple livability, Waterbury remains, as it began, a good place to call home.

"We're still in the infant stage of Waterbury's renaissance," says developer Ralph Calabrese. "Commercial and industrial growth has been, at times, overwhelming. This can be directly attributed to Waterbury's affordable housing, its easy highway access, and its available labor pool. The changes here continue to be quite significant and very positive."

MANUFACTURING FLOURISHES

With all these attributes, it should not be terribly surprising to see Waterbury and the region come back into its own. Indeed, a number of the very first companies to recognize Waterbury's strength—the early manufacturers—are probably not surprised at all. They're still around and still prospering, although not always in their original form. There are even a few companies in the region that continue to produce those first fruits of Waterbury's labor:

ABOVE AND LEFT: Piecework at the button factory is an arduous task. Photos by Robert Houser

buttons and clocks.

The Waterbury Companies, for instance, began making buttons back in 1812 as part of the city's earliest manufacturing groundswell. During the Civil War the company exemplified perhaps the ultimate in hard-headed business sense by making uniform buttons for both the Union Army and the Army of the Confederacy. Today, the Waterbury Companies still makes buttons, but it also manufactures a great deal more.

Timex, which began life as the Waterbury Clock Company, still maintains its headquarters in the region, in Middlebury. The company in its time has produced watches for artillery gunners in World War I, Mickey Mouse watches, fuse timers, and even several million Polaroid cameras. Today Timex is on an upswing. "Compared with five years ago, we're almost an entirely new company," says President Jim Binns.

But manufacturing in Waterbury today extends far beyond buttons and watches and into every imaginable area of endeavor. Although the old ka-chuck, ka-chuck of the brass mills that used to echo through the valley is no longer heard, and factory whistles no longer punctuate the days, many old-line companies continue to flourish as they capitalize on the region's generations-old ability to make things and make them well.

Anamet, for instance, traces its heritage through a complicated industrial family tree back to the earliest brassmakers, and today—after being bought out by its managers earlier in this decade—still numbers among its many operations the production of a variety of metal hose products.

Bristol Babcock Inc., another senior manufacturer, reawoke with a start several years ago, moved into a new Watertown plant, and began producing computer-operated controllers for the gas industry; Risdon, Inc., with operations in Naugatuck and Thomaston, is the world's largest producer of cosmetics and toiletries packaging; and the Eastern Company extends its nineteenth century roots into the twenty-first century with iron and steel production in its Alloy Foundries Division.

The area's manufacturing profile contains a vast array of middle-

ABOVE: A button-blazing machine is in operation inside the Waterbury Companies. Photo by Georgia Sheron

LEFT: John Houlihan is a product designer at the Timex Corporation in Middlebury. Photo by Robert Houser

RIGHT: Workers at the Alcort plant place tremendous emphasis on a high-polished shine. Photo by Georgia Sheron

aged companies as well, whose variety and strength amply demonstrate the talents of the workers involved.

Sailfish and Sunfish, the small and highly popular sailboats, are produced at the AMF-Alcort plant in Waterbury, some 30 years after Al Bryan and Cort Heyniger sailed their wooden prototype on the placid waters of Lake Quassapaug in Middlebury. Chocolate lovers should note that Mounds, Almond Joy, and the rest of the Peter Paul line are produced in great number at the Cadbury-Schweppes plant in Naugatuck. Duracell batteries and Hamilton Beach products also bear, in part at least, a regional imprint, while Alexander Calder often turned to Segre's Iron Works in Waterbury to produce his large iron sculptures.

INDUSTRIAL PARKS AND REDEVELOPMENT

This manufacturing tradition is carried on as well in the region's many industrial parks, all of which have shown signs of flourishing during the economic boom of the late 1980s. Notably successful parks are located in Cheshire, in Watertown, and in Naugatuck, while three have their homes in Waterbury itself. The parks, a number of which still have room for expansion, provide tenants with good access, utilities, and provide for other needs, while sometimes also offering a package of state- and locally-funded incentives to those coming in.

The most gratifying recent news in manufacturing circles around Waterbury may be that high-tech practitioners are also finding the Naugatuck Valley an accommodating home for their ventures. The reasons for this are legion. One important reason is undoubtedly the state's willingness to provide small manufacturers and entrepreneurs with financial support and other incentives. But an attraction

FACING PAGE: Welding is a craft which has been passed on through generations of Waterbury residents. Photo by Georgia Sheron

RIGHT: An inspection takes place along Anamet's corrugated hose assembly line. Photo by Robert Houser

BELOW: Corrugated bronze hose awaits shipment at the Anamet warehouse. Photo by Robert Houser

Cauzin Company, located on South Main Street, produces Soft-strip and other computer-related products. Photo by Georgia Sheron

for these high-tech firms must also be Waterbury's well-trained and well-attuned work force and the abundance of good manufacturing space that is affordable and ready for use.

Cauzin Systems, for example, moved from Norwalk into a Waterbury building that once housed a maker of brass buttons for Union soldiers in the War of 1812. In this space Cauzin produces strip readers that enable users to store and distributed computerized data in compact form.

In Naugatuck, the old U.S. Rubber footwear plant has made way for some 2,000 workers for General DataComm, which moved into the valley from Danbury and which produces modems, data sets, multiplexers, and other items whose names do not appear in dictionaries that are more than five years old.

Some of the massive old manufacturing buildings find themselves today hosting a whole variety of ventures. A dozen or so tenants now occupy the enormous Chase Manufacturing building along the river in Waterville. The building is now known as the Waterbury Industrial Commons, and its occupants produce everything from paper boxes to, in the case of Intermagnetics General Corp., imaging scanners and high-strength superconducting wire.

The old Princeton Knitting Mill in Watertown has similarly been developed by the Siemon Company to become the Princeton Center, a remarkably up-to-date facility offering flexible space for research, light manufacturing, and corporate offices. The center is equipped with state-of-the-art communications equipment as well as access to a CAD/CAM computer system on a time-share, as-needed basis.

Perhaps the most instructive example of this redevelopment phenomenon is the current status of the old Scovill Manufacturing complex on the east end of Waterbury. It is the largest industrial complex in New England, having grown from its humble, one-horse origins in 1802 to 90 buildings on 90 acres and some 2.7 million square feet of floor space that, at its height, employed some 15,000 brass workers.

Scovill is, of course, long gone, having cleared out of its manufacturing plant and its corporate headquarters before disappearing altogether in a puff of takeover smoke. But the hustle and bustle of

business is gradually returning to East Main Street.

New Waterbury Ltd. is the owner of the complex now, and New Waterbury is what it's now called. In place of one major company, the space is now occupied by about 20 tenants, as varied in nature as the city's Health Department, the local chapter of the American Cancer Society, and Rostra Engineered Components, Inc., which occupies some 800,000 square feet, busily following in the footsteps of its brassmaking forebears.

New Waterbury's marketing strategy works well for itself, but it also points out strengths typical of other, similar sites in the region that wish to entice light manufacturing, warehousing, distribution, and other service industries. The first strength is its location, which provides overnight access to the entire Northeast. Second is the variety and adaptability of the space, which ranges from a 2,500-square-foot tool shop to a former strip mill that occupies 20 acres and is the largest industrial building in New England.

The Scovill plant offers such extraordinary features as 20- or 30-foot-high ceilings, overhead cranes, huge service elevators, fireproof vaults, and enormous delivery bays. There is also office space available throughout the complex, much of which offers custom detailing that new office buildings just can't match.

Intermagnetics General Corporation produces imaging scanners and high-strength superconducting wire. Photo by Georgia Sheron

Carl Siemon is the president of Siemon Company, developers of such projects as the Princeton Company. Photo by Georgia Sheron

At $3 or $4 per square foot for industrial use and $8 to $12 for office space, the ultimate Waterbury advantage is most emphatically revealed: It costs less.

Further use of existing buildings (and construction of new ones) should be made possible by the recent designation of Waterbury as the home of one of Connecticut's Enterprise Zones. Companies that are willing to locate within the 1,200 acre zone, which basically runs alongside the Naugatuck River from the Watertown line south to Naugatuck, will receive a number of tax breaks and other incentives. Connecticut, which originated the concept of the Enterprise Zone in order to bring out the dormant potential of urban areas, has enjoyed great success with the scheme. In the five years of their existence, the Enterprise Zones have attracted more that $148 million in investments in 627 projects that have created or retained some 9,400 jobs within the state.

Already, 116 firms that employ some 4,600 people exist within the Waterbury Enterprise Zone, but the area can easily handle further growth.

"The thing that separates Waterbury from most other cities in Connecticut is that it can handle expansion and it can help the area as a whole handle growth," according to Harold W. Smith, Jr., executive vice president of First Federal Savings and Loan of Waterbury.

In the city of Watertown, this worker operates with an injection mold die and a lexan plastic wire-guide. Photo by Robert Houser

Our services are superb in this city. We have a water delivery system that may be one of the best in the world. We have one of the finest fire departments in the country in terms of money lost to fire and catastrophe. Our streets and highways remain relatively uncrowded. In all, we're very well positioned to take advantage of whatever comes our way.

A REGIONAL HUB

And what comes Waterbury's way next should, by all indications, be its emergence as a center for the expanding service sector. Despite its continuing manufacturing strength, the city and region are facing what might be considered the beginning of its second great transformation.

"Our manufacturing side is doing very well," says Frank Fulco, president of the Greater Waterbury Chamber of Commerce.

When people think of Waterbury they think of making things, and that's fine, that's our heritage. But it also seems inevitable that this region will soon experience tremendous growth in service-related jobs. The I-84 and Route 8 corridors are growth corridors. Over the next few years you'll see more Fortune 500 companies moving into the area, more corporate headquarters of all kinds. IBM has become a serious partner with the area beyond *the research and development operation in Southbury It's really just a matter of location more than anything else.*

John Burke, president of Centerbank, feels a tremendous responsibility to the region and is pleased with the progress being made. Photo by Georgia Sheron

And while outlying towns such as Southbury and Watertown, for example, continue to shift and grow, Waterbury has regained its traditional role as the hub—the supplier to the region of wholesale and retail goods and of services as disparate as construction, health care, education, and financial needs.

"I came into Waterbury ten years ago and I bought Starbuck-Sprague, which had first been established in town during the 1920s," says Helmuth Schultze, president of the firm that distributes electrical supplies, factory automation equipment, and commercial and residential lighting. "The city was really down ten years ago, but I saw opportunity here," Schultze continues,

I saw a stable community with lots of room for growth and with an excellent potential, and I saw us growing with it. I would have to say that, based on our success and the way the future looks, Waterbury has indeed turned out to be the place to be, especially and most recently for distributors and for the service sector. I see the city's role not only as the hub to the region, which is where the backbone of my business is now, but as the hub to the entire state.

Schultze has recently moved Starbuck-Sprague into a large new facility on Bank Street in Waterbury, reflecting his commitment to the area and to the city. This is a story that repeats itself many times over these days.

J.E. Smith & Co., a lumber and building supply center and a Waterbury institution since 1897, recently underwent a significant expansion and remodeling of its facility.

"We feel that in Waterbury we are at the center of the wheel," says John McG. Smith, company president. "Obviously, in our business transportation is the key; we have to get materials into Waterbury and then we have to get them distributed throughout all of western Connecticut. All the roads as they exist now and as they are planned make Waterbury the logical place from which to operate."

"In fact," adds Smith, illustrating his point most graphically, "we've just purchased a business that is currently located in New Haven and the first thing we'll do is move it up to Waterbury precisely for the reasons I've just outlined."

The list goes on of expanding or relocating distributors and service sector firms as the new economic tide washes over the region. Torrington Supply Co., a major distributor of plumbing supplies, is creating its own industrial park of refurbished and new buildings on North Elm Street in Waterbury; Crystal Rock Spring Water and United Parcel Service have both made Watertown a key distribution point; Meyers Supply Co. distributes its patent medicines from the Naugatuck Industrial Park; while, in general, computer-related and real estate businesses have mushroomed tremendously in recent years.

WILLING FINANCIAL INSTITUTIONS

And of course the banks have prospered as well. Much of what office expansion downtown Waterbury has seen in the 1980s has been due to the growth of the city's financial institutions, whose hard work, money, and faith in the region have combined to play an important role in Waterbury's resurgence.

"We had a responsibility to the city and the area, and of course

we had a responsiblity to our shareholders and depositors," says
John P. Burke, president of Waterbury-based Centerbank,

*but it's still gratifying to see the progress that's been made. When
you look at downtown Waterbury these days, you see a true financial center that offers its services not only to the outlying towns,
but well beyond. The financial community has greatly increased its
level of services and its sophistication over the past ten years, and,
at the same time, other, outside banks have shown an increased interest in this part of Connecticut.*

A glance at downtown Waterbury shows the huge stake the
banks have invested in the city in recent years—and how well those
investments are paying off. Of the city's native banks, First Federal
Savings and Loan Association of Waterbury has its striking building

*The brass doors of the Centerbank
building are covered with a series
of elaborate details. Here, finance
is highlighted. Photo by Georgia
Sheron*

on the corner of Bank and Grand streets, the Bank of Boston Connecticut's headquarters now occupy four buildings along West Main
Street, Centerbank has spread its offices throughout the central
business district, the Bank of Waterbury enjoys a new headquarters
on Bank Street, and Security Savings and Loan Association is looking
to open a new headquarters in the so-called Pathmark Plaza, also on
Bank Street.

In addition, financial institutions such as Citytrust, Connecticut
Bank and Trust, Connecticut National Bank, United Bank and Trust,
and Society for Savings have also seen the wisdom of expanding their
reach into the Waterbury region.

"We are happy to be playing a role in this area's resurgence," says
Eugene Shugrue, vice president and manager of commercial loans at
Connecticut National Bank. "I think Waterbury's move forward shows
what can happen when you retain your basic values, when you keep
your neighborhoods in order, your commitment to family life in
order, and when you are proud of who you are and where you came
from. I guess what it really comes down to is people."

And, of course, it is people who are the essentials behind all the
statistics and all the talk of revival. It is the people who man the factories, who produce the goods, and who deliver them. It is the people

First Federal Savings is just one of several financial institutions in Waterbury. Photo by Georgia Sheron

who make or break a place like Waterbury, and who, in this case, stand now to be rewarded for their perseverance and faith.

"The people in this city are most definitely the key," says Jaci Carroll, who for over a decade has seen Waterburians come and go at her downtown employment and training establishment.

The people here are solid workers, loyal workers, and they still believe in the work ethic. We've had many cases of employers leaving the region because they thought they could get cheaper labor someplace else, and they could *get cheaper labor; they just couldn't get them to work! You don't have that problem here.*

And so Greater Waterbury stands at the threshhold of the

Local firefighters return to the truck with their hoses, following a minor conflagration. Photo by Georgia Sheron

RIGHT: Police officer Jim Wyrick is proud to work for the City of Waterbury. Photo by Georgia Sheron

FACING PAGE: The Waterbury Chamber of Commerce is located on North Main Street. Photo by Georgia Sheron

1990s, with growing strength and prosperity and a confident outlook that simply didn't exist a decade ago. Its economy is wisely diversified and its fortunes now rest in manufacturing and in the service sector, a balance that should buffer any future ups and downs in the economy at large.

"We stand ready for whatever comes our way," says Chamber of Commerce President Fulco. "We are absolutely in the best shape we've been in for a long, long time. Waterbury has returned to its former glory, reborn in every sense of the word. And as Waterbury has always done in the past, we invite others to come and join us."

Surprising Waterbury

> *The city is thriving . . . I look out the window here, and I see a place that is confident and that is growing and developing in many ways.* CHRISTOPHER BROOKS

If the Waterbury region began as a good home some 315 years ago, it remains one today. Its many charms—both obvious and subtle—are of course best known to those who live there already, but in recent years the region has begun to open up and radiate for visitors and would-be residents who have been drawn to it, usually by the relatively low cost of land and housing. Indeed, today there is little doubt that Greater Waterbury is the part of Connecticut most likely to surprise—and attract—those who come to it for the first time.

The 13-town region is set in a green and prosperous part of the world, in a pleasant area of wooded, rolling hills, enriched with lakes and streams. The terrain comprises much of what is pleasing to the eye about New England, from the striking Metacomet Ridge rising up out of the Central Connecticut Plain to the east, to the Naugatuck Valley, with its ravines and impressive crags, to the lush Pomperaug Valley, and the postcard beauty of the Berkshire foothills as they march off to the northwest.

The region's climate is temperate, and the weather, as Mark Twain once noted, is changeable, with conditions influenced to some degree by both the nearby ocean and the higher ground to the north. The four seasons are distinct but not unusually severe, as a rule, and each offers its own pleasures, be it winter skiing on a Woodbury slope, springtime trout fishing in a Bethlehem stream, a summer afternoon's sail on Middlebury's Lake Quassapaug, or all the well-documented joys of autumn in New England.

AN ENVIABLE QUALITY OF LIFE

But while the four seasons can highlight much that is pleasurable within the region, there is also a nearness to much of what is truly great and widely envied in American life and culture.

"The thing about Waterbury," says Michael McKeeman, a city resident, "is that if you've got a weekend or a short vacation coming up and you don't want to stick around, you've got an easy drive to places that are really world-class and world renowned. Last week I was trying to decide if I wanted to go to Newport or to Saratoga Springs, and I ended up driving to Fenway Park in Boston for a Red Sox game."

In fact, within two-hour range by car or train are such varied diversions as a Broadway play, a Vermont ski mountain, the Rhode Island surf beaches, an outdoor concert at Tanglewood in the Berkshires, an autumn day at West Point, or the contests of any one of more than a dozen major professional sports teams.

An hour's drive or less covers virtually all of Connecticut, including nationally acclaimed regional theaters; the cultural and educational programs of Connecticut's superb universities, most notably Yale and all its related activities in New Haven; the attractions of the Hartford Civic Center, especially the Hartford Whalers, Big East college basketball, and the Boston Celtics; and the sophisticated dining

and shopping, the weekend hideaways, and the diverse recreation that have all long been a part of life in Connecticut.

But as pleasing as the excursions may be, and as often as the urge to partake in them might be indulged, most people come to Greater Waterbury because that is where they want to stay; that is where they want their home to be. And certainly all that is great in the traditions and in the civilization of Connecticut can be found in the 13-town region. There is a sense of peace and stability in the town greens and white-steepled churches, in the stone walls and pastures that are so common to the area. There is strength and vitality and renewed economic life in the manufacturing towns and retail centers of the valley.

And at the center of it all sits Waterbury, in every sense prepared to seize its role as the vital hub of the region. Its many strengths as a center for business have already been noted, but its strengths as a place in which to live are equally impressive.

Waterbury is built on a series of hills, and these hills are easily the city's dominant physical characteristic. While the hills may give snowplowers pause every once in a while in winter, they also create wonderful views and evoke a very strong and resonant sense of place. Because of the terrain, according to historian William J. Pape writing in 1918, "Waterbury is ideally located for architectural effects. Its wooded hills, rising gradually from a wide basin, have given its builders and designers opportunities of which they were not slow

FACING PAGE: The Chase Municipal Building represents strength and confidence for many proud residents of Waterbury. Photo by Barry Rabinowitz

PAGES 70-71: Yale University, in New Haven, occupies the majority of the buildings visible in the foreground of this image, and much, much more. Photo by Jack McConnell

BELOW: When trout season opens in Southbury, one can hardly find room for a foothold in the river. Photo by Georgia Sheron

to take advantage. There has never been any serious opposition to the widening of important thoroughfares, nor to the erection of city buildings of which its people may well be proud. No finer architectural effects can be found in New England . . ."

HISTORY SHAPES THE URBAN CORE

What is remarkable today is how many of those effects have survived, and how they still, all these years later, continue to define the city. The handsome core of Waterbury and many of its surrounding residences remain essentially intact from the early decades of this cen-

White-steepled churches and autumn foliage dot this downtown aerial of Woodbury. Photo By Jack McConnell

tury, giving the city not only a fine architectural stock, but also giving its citizens a sense of permanence and continuity that is increasingly precious in a fast-changing world.

A short trip down Grand Street and then to the Green is most instructive of this. At the west end of Grand Street stands Waterbury's most distinctive landmark, the tower of the old Union Station. The building, designed by the renowned firm of McKim, Mead and White, and completed in 1909, has a fascinating history. Around the turn of the century, C.W. Mellon, president of the New York, New Haven & Hartford Railroad, went on a trip to Italy, where he and his wife were greatly impressed by the famous Campanile in Siena. At the first board meeting following his return to this country, Mellon suggested that the next station to be built by the railroad be modeled after the tower he had so admired in Italy. And so it is (and such was the power of the railroads in those days) that Waterbury got its magnificent rail depot and surely one of the most splendid clock towers in America.

Across the street from the station is the old American Brass headquarters, a building designed by Trowbridge and Livingston of New York and built in 1913. The building, whose ornate brass doors are

a particular delight, was contructed along a partial crescent in order to follow the sweep of lower Grand Street (and as such is unfailingly a marvel to young boys and girls who are seeing it for the first time).

Further along the street, past the distinctive Silas Bronson Library, the Superior Court (both designed by Waterbury architect Joseph Stein), and the Southern New England Telephone Company building, there sits a remarkable five-building cluster that is the work of noted American architect Cass Gilbert, who also designed the U.S. Supreme Court building and the Woolworth Building in New York. Gilbert's Waterbury buildings began with the city hall and the

Three churches on the New Haven green face City Hall and the harbor beyond. Photo by Jack McConnell

Hartford after dark remains alive with activity. Photo by Jack McConnell

limestone-and-granite Chase Building directly across the street, and they continued with the old Waterbury National Bank building and two smaller buildings on adjacent Field Street.

The western end of Grand Street features the art deco John S. Monagan Federal Building and, across the street, a block of commercial buildings dating from the first decade of this century, whose facades reflect just about every architectural style popular during that era.

The block-long trip to the Green from Grand Street can be made by Church Street, Leavenworth Street, or Bank Street, each alive with activity and each featuring structures of significance, ranging from old downtown mansions to a dozen or so restored commercial buildings.

The Green itself is a popular gathering place, as it has been since the city began. Over the centuries it has served many purposes: as the first common ground for the early settlers, as a grazing pasture for cattle and sheep, as an elm-shaded retreat for an industry-

weary populace, and, today, as Waterbury's central park, where the
city's ideas and its business—and many of its most colorful characters—
crisscross every day. The Green was, is, and always will be Waterbury's heart—the place for great public events, where Presidents,
presidential candidates, and orators both official and unofficial traditionally have come to be heard. It is also alleged by certain Waterbury
natives that if you drink the water from the Carrie Welton Fountain
(the Green's famous "horse" fountain), you are destined one day to
return to the city.

The buildings that surround the Green are, for the most part,
stately and well-proportioned. Most notable are the stone-steepled St.
John's Church, the awesome Renaissance basilica of the Church of
the Immaculate Conception, the pyramid-topped Mattatuck Museum,
the Elton Building, and the Centerbank Building. To the north, the
buildings of the Green blend into the houses that make up the historic Hillside District, a remarkable jumble of residences—mostly in

The lawn of the Connecticut State Capitol in Hartford provides a pleasant repose, for both business people and tourists. Photo by Jack McConnell

the Queen Anne, Victorian, or Colonial styles—that once served as homes for the city's rich and famous.

All of this adds up to a downtown of uncommon distinction, especially as new buildings and refurbished old ones continue to come into play along East Main Street, South Main Street, and lower Bank Street. Urban historian Matthew Roth has claimed that Waterbury contains "the best examples of late 19th and early 20th century urban architecture in Connecticut." That sentiment was echoed by noted Connecticut photographer Charles Reich, who says of Waterbury, "For me, it's like walking into a museum."

A CITY OF CONCERN

True enough, except that this "museum" is roaring with activity. The buildings so admired by architectural experts are alive inside not only with businesses and commercial establishments, but also with

many of the institutions that distinguish a city and make it a whole and civilizing place.

Churches, for instance, have always been an integral part of Waterbury's landscape, and today is no exception. From the earliest churches of the seventeenth and early eighteenth centuries, the religious community in Waterbury has grown to include some 90 churches and some 30 faiths and denominations. While the city remains largely Roman Catholic due to large Irish and Italian populations (in fact, earlier in this century Waterbury was known as the "City of Priests" for the large number of its young men who entered the priesthood), its ethnic diversity has always meant it has been home to an unusually high number of different faiths and beliefs.

Organizations devoted to youth were also quick to take root in Waterbury, and many of them have flourished for years. Many small neighborhood organizations, mostly devoted to athletics, add vitality

A Sunday drive along quiet country roads within greater Waterbury proves very relaxing. Photo by Jack McConnell

FACING PAGE: Lovely surprises await those who take the time to explore Waterbury. Photo by Jack McConnell

Country flavor surrounds Waterbury. Photo by Jack McConnell

to local parks and clubhouses, while citywide football, basketball, and baseball leagues are well-organized and highly popular.

"I think that if you are going to have a city that is a family place, which Waterbury certainly is, then you are going to see a great many programs and facilities that are designed for kids," says John Donahue, a city alderman and cofounder of Friends of Fulton Park. "The people here seem to guard their programs jealously. They see what happens in other cities when things are allowed to deteriorate."

On a larger scale, the Waterbury YMCA, one of the first to be established in the nation, has grown to become a formidable presence

Old Union Station possesses Waterbury's most distinctive landmark; this clock tower, modeled after the Campanile in Siena. Photo by Jack McConnell

on the Green, with two pools, two gyms, and a variety of other facilities and programs for young people and adults as well, especially, it seems, the army of runners who pour out of the "Y"'s doors every noon-time and onto the city streets. Also part of the downtown scene and firmly a part of the city's culture are the Waterbury YWCA, the Waterbury Girls Club, the Waterbury Boys Club, the Pearl Street Community Center, the Libra Athletic Club, and a host of other organizations, mostly devoted to city youth.

Other institutions that give the city strength include the large number of social and civic associations, whether they be formed for ethnic, religious, athletic, fraternal, or philanthropic reasons. The ethnic organizations range from the elaborate Pontelandolfo Club on its own acreage in the Lakewood section of town to the Cape Verdean Social Club at the head of Cherry Street, just off North Square. The athletic, social, and fraternal organizations range from the Waterbury Country Club, with its splendid 18-hole golf course, to the many fraternal clubs whose presence gives a boost and some backbone to many city activities.

Sheep and cattle were once pastured on the Waterbury Green. Photo by Jack McConnell

Chief among the philanthropic organizations is the Waterbury Foundation, which was established locally to provide assistance in areas where traditional help is not available.

"Our assets have more than doubled in the last five years to over $5 million, greatly increasing our ability to be of service to the community," notes Christopher Brooks, the Foundation's president. "That's a good sign for Waterbury as a whole, I think. It tells me that the city is thriving and that its people are supporting the institutions, such as ours, that can help the city to rise above the ordinary

LEFT: *This horse fountain, known as the Carrie Welton Fountain, is located on the Green. Photo by Barry Rabinowitz*

BELOW: *One of several significant buildings surrounding the Green is the Mattatuck Museum. Photo by Georgia Sheron*

Queen Anne, Colonial, and Victorian homes blend together to comprise the historic Hillside District. Photo by Georgia Sheron

and help those in need. I look out the window here," Brooks says from his office above the Green, "and I see a place that is confident and that is growing and developing in many ways."

MEDIA/EDUCATION/HEALTH CARE

Much of the city's development is due to its exposure to the world at large, not only through its own population, but also through its location near the center of the world's most intensive media market.

The local media have traditionally served the city and the region well. There are two daily newspapers—*The Waterbury Republican* and *The American*—both under the longtime ownership of the Pape family and published since the 1960s from the old railroad station, with bureaus in some of the outlying towns. The city is also home to three AM radio stations—WATR, WWCO, and WQQW, all of which have a strong local flavor—and two FM stations, WWYZ and WIOF, which seek a statewide audience. Waterbury also is home to one television station, the independent WTXX, Channel 20.

But beyond this very substantial local media, Waterbury's location also places it squarely in the middle of media heaven. A downtown newsstand will routinely carry all the New York newspapers, daily papers from four or five other Connecticut cities, two dailies from Boston, as well as various weeklies and national papers. The cable companies that serve the region all carry channels from New York and Boston, while the tremendous variety of the Northeast is available across the radio dial.

"People from Waterbury are sometimes accused of being too interested in local matters and not enough in the rest of the world," says city assessor Michael Moriarty. "But I don't think it's a matter of provincialism. The people of Waterbury are very informed and very aware of the rest of the world. It's just that the characters you find in the rest of the world don't quite match up to the ones you find in Waterbury."

Waterbury remains strong in other of life's fundamentals as

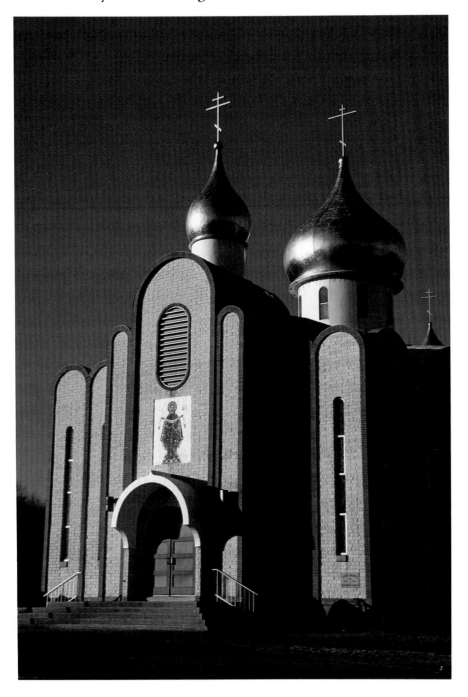

Saint Mary's Orthodox Church provides a strong visual contrast to the typical New England-style white steepled chapels. Photo by Georgia Sheron

well. The public school system, for instance, remains significantly superior to most other systems in Connecticut's large cities, while some of the school systems in the region are among the very best in the state. Connecticut's Education Enhancement Act, which greatly increased teacher salaries in the state, seems to have been tailored expressly for cities like Waterbury, where more qualified candidates are applying to jobs and teacher morale has rebounded—all to the ultimate benefit of the city's school children.

Waterbury's public schools—19 elementary, three middle schools, and three high schools—are buttressed by a strong system of parochial schools. The 10 Catholic elementary schools and two high schools have long been influential in the education of Waterbury's young. In addition, Kaynor Vocational and Technical School has been instrumental in producing the highly skilled workers who have for so long been responsible for the city's worldwide reputation.

The city has become a center for higher education, to the benefit of undergraduates and adults who seek new skills or who simply wish to expand their horizons. The University of Connecticut has a branch located in Waterbury, while the new Higher Education Center on the west side of town combines the facilities of both Mattatuck Community College and Waterbury State Technical College into a single resource that is of tremendous use to the city and the

ABOVE: Public safety is an ongoing concern of local government, thus the National Guard Armory is well maintained. Photo by Barry Rabinowitz

FACING PAGE: Saint John's Church, with its stone steeple, presides over the Green. Photo by Barry Rabinowitz

Security Savings Bank sponsored this children's road race. Photo by Barry Rabinowitz

This student of Waterbury Technical College catches up on some work in the computer lab. Photo by Georgia Sheron

region. Waterbury is also home to Post College, a private four-year school that has grown and prospered along with the city in recent years, and now offers more than 1,700 full- and part-time students both associate and bachelor's degree programs.

Finally, Greater Waterbury is in the midst of a superb network of private secondary schools and universities that not only provide unparalleled educations for their students, but which also often make their facilities and programs available to the general public. Notable secondary schools include St. Margaret's-McTernan School in Waterbury, Taft in Watertown, Westover in Middlebury, and Cheshire Academy in Cheshire. Not much farther afield are a whole galaxy of prep schools—

The Taft School is dusted with snow following a midwinter storm. Photo by Georgia Sheron

including Kent, Hotchkiss, Choate, Canterbury, and Westminster—that consistently rank among the very best in the nation. Yale, Wesleyan, Trinity, the University of Hartford, Fairfield University, and the University of Bridgeport are all within 40 minutes of downtown Waterbury.

The city is exceptionally well-served in matters of health care as well. Waterbury Hospital and St. Mary's Hospital are major facilities that have reliably tended to the city's and region's health needs for many years. Each hospital has undergone major expansion in recent years, and combined they provide the region with some 900 beds in modern and well-equipped facilities.

A GROWING CULTURAL FORCE

Finally, Waterbury is also reclaiming its ancient mantle as the cultural hub for the area. While much in the way of arts and culture exists nearby, Waterbury itself has more to offer than it has in years.

The Mattatuck Museum, on West Main Street downtown, is the

At the Waterbury Arts Festival, this ballerina danced her way into the hearts of many. Photo by Barry Rabinowitz

city's foremost cultural gem. The museum is newly housed in the former Masonic Temple, with renovations designed by the internationally known architect Cesar Pelli. The building, with its distinctive copper ziggurat rising over a brick and limestone entryway, now provides the architectural finishing touch at the northwest corner of the Green, and it includes a garden courtyard, a cafe, and a gift shop.

Also inside the museum are spacious, newly renovated gallery spaces that house special exhibits and an extensive collection of paintings and sculpture by Connecticut artists that include John Trumbull, Frederick Church, and Alexander Calder. In addition, an updated and fascinating walk-through historical exhibit tells the story of everyday life in the region, from the time of the first settlers to the present century.

"We are very proud of the new Mattatuck Museum," says museum director Ann Smith. "Our hope is that it reflects the city around it and that it will be a vital resource and a useful neighbor for the people who live in the region. Just as Waterbury is a pleasant surprise for a lot of visitors, so is the museum."

The museum offers a number of cultural, artistic, and educational programs for adults and children. It also offers occasional walking tours and brochures outlining bicycle and walking trips throughout the city.

On the other end of the Green, on East Main Street, another venerable cultural institution is getting a facelift. The Palace Theatre, a spectacular marble and gilt temple to entertainment built in the early 1920s, is being brought back to its full splendor, thanks to a multimillion-dollar renovation effort. The Palace is expected to be instrumental in making Waterbury once again a center for the performing arts, with concerts, drama, and dance planned for the big stage and 3,000-seat arena.

"The Palace is an awesome theater with a wonderful history," says Anthony Bergin, chairman of the Greater Waterbury Visitors and Convention Bureau. "If it can be booked well and promoted effectively, it can really help lead Waterbury back into the cultural limelight."

Among the local cultural groups who are looking forward to being a part of the new Palace are the Waterbury Symphony Orchestra, the Waterbury Chorale, and perhaps even the newly formed Water-

The Waterbury Symphony Orchestra performs with vigor. Photo by Georgia Sheron

LEFT: Food booths are an essential ingredient to local festivities. Courtesy, Waterbury Convention and Visitors Commission

FACING PAGE: This arbor of roses is located at Elizabeth Park. Photo by Jack McConnell

bury Opera Theater Company—three organizations that reflect the city's (and the region's) longtime appreciation of and support for the arts.

One of the newer and more innovative cultural occasions in Waterbury is the Waterbury Ethnic Music Festival, which for the past several years has celebrated the rich cultural mix that exists in the city. Organized by historian Jeremy Brecher following his research into the city's musical heritage, the Festival has provided all comers with a taste of Greek, Irish, Lithuanian, German, Yiddish, French, Puerto Rican, and African music, to name a few.

Another recent and successful addition to the city's cultural scene is the Waterbury Festival, which each September has combined, on city streets and in Library Park, the remnants of the old Waterbury Arts Festival with a food festival that features foods from area restaurants. The combination of good food and good music has proved wildly successful, as it invariably does.

The city and the region are notably partial to good food anyway, as any place with strong links to the Old World ought to be. During the 1970s and 1980s, Waterbury experienced a noticeable boom in restaurant start-ups that in many respects was at the forefront of the city's overall revival. The emphasis in the city and in the area is on Italian cuisine, with such notable Waterbury establishments as Faces, 1249, and the No Fish Today Cafe providing not only wonderful food, but also an atmosphere that is distinctly Waterbury. (In fact, it is said that a night of perfect enjoyment, Waterbury style, is dinner at the No Fish followed by live jazz at the Hillside Restaurant on Willow Street.)

But the restaurant boom in Waterbury goes well beyond Italian food to include, for instance, excellent fish and seafood at the

BELOW: Good food and drink are available at the Westside Lobster House, located in the Hotel Elton. Photo by Georgia Sheron

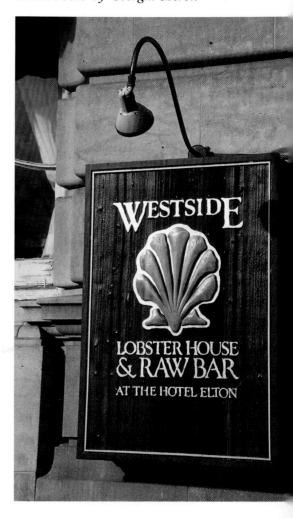

Westside Lobster House, a first-class grill at The Hills, and a very rich treasure of dining places in the surrounding towns. It also includes superb pizza at places such as Bacco's and Domenic's, a rapturous hot dog experience (especially on a warm summer evening) at Blackie's in Cheshire, or dinner at any of the city hotels, including the Waterbury Sheraton, the Red Bull Inn, the Downtown Howard Johnson's, or the soon-to-be-completed Crowne Plaza Hotel, also downtown.

All of this would seem to add up to a lot for a city of barely 100,000 persons, yet it still doesn't pinpoint Waterbury's prime attraction as a place to live. That attraction would have to be found somewhere beneath the surface, in the city's many neighborhoods, in its people, and in the heart and soul of the place.

"This has become a very attractive city," says one native who returned several years ago to settle down. "You have a lot of what's so desireable about Connecticut without the ridiculous prices.

"But to me it's attractive for other reasons, too. It's unpretentious. The people are down to earth and they believe in home and family and all those good things that we were all brought up to believe in. But it's not bland and it's definitely not a haven for yuppies. It's just a good combination of things, I guess, and it makes me feel good to be home again."

ABOVE: Main Street in downtown Waterbury is aglow with the late afternoon sun. Photo by Jack McConnell

FACING PAGE: One Waterbury neighborhood includes this street of two family homes. Photo by Jack McConnell

This Favored Region

> Many of the 13 cities that comprise the Waterbury region are being "discovered" for their charm and potential.

Just as much of the strength and vitality of Waterbury comes from the diversity of its people, so does much of the strength of the Waterbury region come from the diversity of the 13 cities and towns that are contained in it. Indeed, nearly all the charms and advantages of life in modern New England can be found within Greater Waterbury's 300 square miles.

Dynamism and new growth are evident in many places within the region, although a "go slow" attitude and a retention of New England charm are not uncommon either. The spirit of rebirth can be felt not only in Waterbury itself, but also in the venerable industrial towns of Naugatuck and Thomaston along the river. The growth is even more evident in several other towns, which are feeling the impact of having been "discovered" for their location, their access to transportation routes, and their quietly sophisticated way of life. Cheshire, Southbury, and Watertown have all experienced recent rapid—but not runaway—growth, from which the entire region has drawn benefits.

Yet through it all the old New England is easy to find, be it in the stone walls of Middlebury, the historic Main Street of Woodbury, or the rural landscapes of Bethlehem. The sense of history, the commitment to the ancient virtues, the importance of family and education remain stubbornly a part of the place.

There is no doubt that a separate book could be written for each of the towns of the region. In most cases, one has. Certainly, each of the towns retains a fierce local identity, nurtured through the centuries and encouraged by Connecticut's tradition of home rule. In several cases, the only similarity between certain towns in

the region is one strictly of geography. But it is precisely this diversity that makes this area so attractive. And each of the 12 towns that surrounds Waterbury has an interesting story to tell.

BEACON FALLS

Beacon Falls straddles the Naugatuck River about seven miles south of Waterbury, its high hills and narrow river passage serving as a natural divider between the upper and lower Naugatuck Valley.

Beacon Falls was first settled in 1678 by colonists moving north from Derby in search of riverine pastures. Prior to white settlement, the region was evidently a much-used Paugasuck Indian encampment, as many relics and arrowheads have been turned up in local soil. What the first settlers found was pastureland suitable only for several farming families, and the area was populated very

PAGES 100-101: A horse-drawn wagon carries local produce to market. Photo by Jack McConnell

BELOW: Sports enthusiasts are jazzed when they can windsurf on Lake Quassapaug late into the fall. Photo by Barry Rabinowitz

*Geraniums and ivy are both
strong, hardy varieties of flora
commonly seen in the Northeast.
Photo by Jack McConnell*

gradually. Indeed, it wasn't until 1871 that Beacon Falls would
be incorporated from lands of Bethany, Naugatuck, Oxford, and
Seymour.

The town participated in the nineteenth-century manufacturing
boom with mixed results. In 1834, Thomas Sanford is said to have
invented the friction match in Beacon Falls, but he went off to
Woodbridge to manufacture it. (In Woodbridge, Sanford occupied a
mill too large for its water source, became discouraged, and sold his
formula for $10 to men who used it to create the Diamond Match
Company.)

In the early 1850s the first Beacon Falls rubber shop produced

Riverine pastures much like this one were highly sought after for settlement. Photo by Jack McConnell.

Marigolds and asters grow along this white picket fence. Photo by Jack McConnell

hard rubber goods like powder flasks, whip sockets, and buttons. After some 10 years of operations, however, the management split off to New York and to Seymour, and the Home Woolen Mill moved into the factory to produce capes and, later, raincoats—neither with notable success. In the 1880s, the Homer D. Bronson Company, located a half-mile south of the old rubber company, began producing fine brass novelty items.

In 1898 the Beacon Falls Rubber Shoe Company was organized and enjoyed success enough so that outlets were soon established in Boston, New York, Chicago, Kansas City, Minneapolis, and San Francisco. In 1918, historian William J. Pape was able to note:

the company maintains a band within its organization which plays selections every noon time the year around, in front of the plant, while in the summer months many concerts are given in the cozy little park fronting on the main street, which are thoroughly enjoyed by the townspeople and oftentimes by automobile parties

from nearby towns. The company is interested in developing a colony of employees owning their own homes in Beacon Falls. A comprehensive plan has been worked out by the company's officials toward that end.

This experiment, and indeed, the company itself, came to an end in 1930, however, when all was absorbed into the U.S. Rubber Company in neighboring Naugatuck.

Today Beacon Falls remains a small, residential town. Its area of 9 square miles makes it the smallest town in Greater Waterbury, and its population is approximately 4,500. In recent years it has become something of a bedroom community; its relatively low real estate prices and easy access to Route 8 make it attractive to commuters from Waterbury, New Haven, and other points.

Beacon Falls' physical attraction, especially along the river, is unquestioned. Much of the most spectacular terrain is now contained in the nearly 2,000-acre Naugatuck State Forest, which rises abruptly some 600 feet on each side of the river. In 1892 J.L. Rockey noted in his *History of New Haven County* that "The rugged Naugatuck Valley is nowhere more picturesque and attractive than in the town of Beacon Falls." This certainly remains true today.

BETHLEHEM

Those who come into the Waterbury region with a yearning for the many charms of a small, rural, altogether lovely New England town will find those virtues best exemplified in the Town of Bethlehem. With only 2,800 residents spread out over some 20 square miles in the hills of Litchfield County, Bethlehem—from its town green to its still-active farmlands—represents much of what is most cherished and celebrated about New England.

In many respects, Bethlehem is a classic Connecticut hill town, isolated throughout its history from primary transportation routes and thus largely self-sufficient, sparsely populated, and devoted to its own affairs.

The isolation was apparent from the very beginning, as one historian noted:

The first settlers [1734] were hardy, enterprising, self-denying men, well qualified to endure the hardships of pioneer life. The women, as well as the men, went on foot, or on horseback, through a trackless wilderness, guided by marked trees. In the midst of the first dreary winter their provisions gave out, and the inhabitants were obliged to thread their way through the pathless forest to the old settlement (Woodbury) for food.

Bethlehem (originally called "Bethlem") was incorporated from Woodbury in 1787. For most of its history since then, the town's pursuits have been largely agricultural. In 1881, a history of Litchfield County could note:

Bethlehem is a small town, with an average length of four and one-half miles, and a breadth of four miles. Its inhabitants are mostly engaged in agricultural pursuits. There is one carriage manufactory, one woolen mill, one store, and blacksmith shops and saw mills to accommodate the public. The land is rolling but fertile, being very suitable for fruit growing. There is a library in the town of nearly twelve hundred volumes, which is well patronized, making an intelligent community.

Today, Bethlehem is notable for the annual Bethlehem Fair, begun in 1936 and now the foremost country fair in the region. It is known for its longstanding nickname of "Christmas Town" and the great volume of holiday mail that goes through the local post office each December; and for the Abbey of Regina Laudis, a cloistered convent whose Little Art Shop has long been a popular source of crafts and local produce.

Most notably, however, Bethlehem best demonstrates that Greater Waterbury is not only *near* the postcard beauty of a small New England town, it actually is a *part* of it. A country ride along Carmel Hill Road at any time of year is a most pleasant immersion into the Connecticut countryside. Similarly, a drive to the top of Todd Hill Road brings the motorist to the highest point in the Waterbury region—some 1,140 feet above sea level—and offers striking views in all directions, including west to the Berkshires and south as far as Long Island Sound.

CHESHIRE

Location has always been a key to Cheshire's growth and prosperity. It was true in the eighteenth century, when Cheshire's main street was a link on the Hartford-New Haven Turnpike and businesses and inns sprang up to cater to the stagecoach trade. It was true in the nineteenth century, when Cheshire's farms and light industry prospered as the Farmington Canal was laid through town on its intended way from the Long Island Sound to Northampton, Massachusetts. And it is true today, as this rapidly growing town presents an ideal combination of industrial, commercial, and residential elements.

Cheshire today, with a population of around 26,000, is a self-contained town in many respects. Residentially, however, its proximity to Hartford, New Haven, and Waterbury, and its many outstanding residential sections, make it a popular bedroom community for commuters. But Cheshire's location on two interstates (I-84 and I-691) has brought diversity as well. At present, the town is home to 10 industrial, business, or commercial parks and such major employers as Airpax, which is involved in electronics; Bendix Corporation, which produces measuring instruments; Bozzuto's, a food distributorship; Bloomingdale's catalogue distribution center; and a research arm of the Olin Corporation. In addition, there are big plans for the area around the intersection of Route 10 (the old Hartford-New Haven Turnpike) and the recently completed I-691: a large, upscale retail center—the Apple Valley Mall—is in the planning stages, as well as a business park, distribution center, and a hotel/office complex.

Another white steeple, the First Congregational Church of Cheshire, is an exceptional work of architecture. Photo by Jack McConnell

All of this seems very far removed from the small farming community that was first settled in 1694 by families from Wallingford who were seeking more inviting pastures in what they called West Farms, on the west side of the Quinnipiac River. Although most of the early settlers were indeed farmers, other pursuits were soon established as well. Primary among these was mining, first for copper and even gold, and later, more profitably, for barite.

According to a history of the town:

The early settlers of old Wallingford were impressed with the belief that their numerous hills abounded with mineral wealth; and the

evidence of the existence of the precious metals were especially abundant in what is now the southeastern part of Cheshire. Here, fine specimens of copper appeared on the surface, which led to the discovery and opening of a mine, some time about 1710.

Although very little copper (or gold) was ever found, the name "Copper Valley" remains in common usage to this day.

Barite was mined from about 1840 to 1880. Large deposits were found in the southeastern and northwestern parts of town as dozens of shafts were sunk to depths of up to 600 feet, and the industry once gave employment to more than 1,000 miners, including several hundred specially imported from Cornwall, England.

But by the end of the century, the mining craze had subsided, the canal had been thoroughly superceded by the railroad, and Cheshire went back to being a quiet farming town. "The valleys . . . are generally very fertile, the soil being a gravelly loam," someone wrote of Cheshire in the 1890s. "On the hills the soil is less rich but is admirably adapted for fruit culture and the grasses. There are some fine orchards and farms—and of all kinds, more than 300 in number—a large proportion of the inhabitants being agriculturists." Of the town center it was written: "The immediate environs, consisting of orchards and fields, dotted with pleasant homes, aid to make

this one of the most attractive villages in the state." And in fact in the early decades of the twentieth century, Cheshire—and its well-known eateries such as the Waverly Inn—became a highly regarded retreat for those seeking to escape New Haven or Waterbury for a country drive and a meal.

FACING PAGE: Picking fresh apples can be a family affair. Photo by Jack McConnell

Although the number of farms has dropped dramatically, Cheshire today still contains popular orchards and other cultivation of the soil, enough so that the town was only recently designated as "The Bedding Capital of Connecticut" —referring to its abundant nurseries and flower farms. It is also home to 18 restaurants, 11 banks, a lively retail section along Route 10, and an exceptional public school system. It is also home to Cheshire Academy, which was established during the 1790s, originally as an alternative to Yale, which was said at that time to discriminate against Episcopalians (supposedly because Episcopalians were, as a group, thought to be loyal to England during the Revolution). The Episcopal Academy of Connecticut, as it was called for many years, never did become a college, but as an academy it has flourished in Cheshire for many years.

And Cheshire has flourished around it. Today, the town enjoys a per-capita income of more than $15,000 and retail sales of more than $600 million, a phenomenal total for a town of its size. With an excellent mix of growth projected for the near future—and with its location within the state nearly perfect—Cheshire can expect to prosper well into the next century.

MIDDLEBURY

The spirit of independence that swept the new nation following the Revolutionary War was keenly felt in Waterbury, as first Watertown, then Wolcott and Oxford, and finally Middlebury broke away to form separate communities. The case of Middlebury was fairly typical. First, the residents sought and were granted "winter privileges," meaning that during the cold, snowy months churchgoers would not have to travel into central Waterbury but instead could arrange for a preacher locally. The next step was to establish an independent church society, which occurred in 1790 when portions of Woodbury, Southbury, and the West Farms portion of Waterbury banded together to form under the logical name of Middlebury. In 1800 the other shoe dropped when the Society of Middlebury petitioned the state General Assembly for an act of town incorporation.

Waterbury objected, as it had with the others, saying, "the effect of dismemberment would be to cut us up into mouthfuls ready for the devourer." Waterbury also contended that many of its fine citizens— most notably members of the Bronson and Porter families—had moved to the western reaches of town and thus would be lost (along with their money) should Middlebury become a separate town. But the trend was well established, and Middlebury was incorporated in 1807, in part, the General Assembly noted, because Middlebury was separated from Waterbury "by a rough and uninhabitable tract of country."

Middlebury today is not often referred to as rough and uninhabitable. Indeed, it has become, for the most part, a classic residential suburb of 6,200 population, with many fine country homes of old and recent vintage, and a very pleasant countryside, yet excellent access to I-84, to Waterbury, and to points beyond. This access is no doubt part of the reason why Middlebury has become home to the corporate headquarters of three major corporations: Timex, Uniroyal, and General DataComm.

Middlebury's most evident physical characteristic is the lovely Lake Quassapaug, which was once the site of satinet mills and a

Autumn brings a wealth of plump pumpkins for harvest. Photo by Jack McConnell

Lake Quassapaug offers boaters the opportunity to hone their skills. Photo by Georgia Sheron

match company, but which today presents an ideal setting for sailing and swimming. While most of the lakeside is lined with woods or cottages, the south end is notable for the Quassy Amusement Park, long a fixture for the Waterbury region. The park was established in 1908 when the Connecticut Company decided to run its trolley through Middlebury on its way from Waterbury to Woodbury. This route (which bypassed a disgruntled Watertown) made Quassy a popular resort, and today it remains one of Connecticut's premier amusement parks; its rides are especially well suited to small children, while its picnic areas and outing sheds are used by area organizations.

One of Middlebury's other well-known institutions was begun at virtually the same time as Quassy Park. Westover School was established in 1908 and opened in 1909 by Mary Robbins Hillard, who

had previously been in charge of St. Margaret's School for Girls in Waterbury. Miss Hillard's stated goal was a "thorough and systematic education" for her charges, and with the help of J.H. Whittemore, a magnificent school building—designed by Miss Theodate Pope—was erected on the south end of Middlebury's quiet town center. The school was an immediate success and it quickly established itself as one of the best girls' schools in the country, which it remains today.

NAUGATUCK

The fortunes of Naugatuck and Waterbury have long been intertwined. Although it has only about a quarter of Waterbury's population, Naugatuck's economic story line follows the same ups and downs, from its beginning as a rather unsuccessful farming community and its emergence as a manufacturing center, to its smothering embrace by a single industry, its decline in the 1960s and 1970s, and its recent upturn in fortunes due to a more stable and diversified economic base. In fact, the opportunities that exist today in Naugatuck—the relatively low real estate prices, the able work force, the ample manufacturing space—echo all along the Valley, most notably in Waterbury.

Naugatuck was first settled in 1703, when Samuel Hickox of Farmington strayed south of Waterbury to build a house and begin farming. The settlement grew very little during the ensuing years; in fact, Salem Society was not established as the first parish until 1773. Some use was made of the settlement's ample waterpower during the early years of the nineteenth century, and, gradually, concerns that produced clocks, tinware, buttons, and cutlery sprang up.

Naugatuck's enormous leap forward came in January 1839, when one of its citizens, Charles Goodyear, finally hit upon the formula that would properly "vulcanize" rubber and thus open that substance up to a world of uses. Goodyear was a driven inventor and a hapless soul, born in New Haven in 1800, who for years sought with an admirable (if rather self-destructive) single-mindedness to make rubber a commercially profitable commodity. Along the way, he suffered through bankruptcy and intense privation, and he came up with unlikely products like a rubber desk ornately trimmed with gold-leafed ormulu, and hard rubber gold-handled canes, both of which took silver medals at London's Crystal Palace Exhibit—but which won no medals with the public at large.

When Goodyear hit upon the correct formula, however, all of Naugatuck hit with him. The Goodyear India Rubber Shoe Company opened its doors in 1843 and it quickly became the largest producer of rubber footwear in the world. While Goodyear himself went on to experience continued misfortune, poverty, and an early death, Naugatuck prospered. It was granted incorporation in 1844, with land

FACING PAGE: Warm autumn color surrounding this barn in Middlebury is reflected in the lake below. Photo by Jack McConnell

taken from Waterbury, Bethany, and Oxford. Its population, fueled in great part by the health of the rubber industry, jumped from 1,720 in 1850 to 10,541 in 1900.

During the first half of the present century, Naugatuck was readily identified worldwide as a major manufacturer of rubber goods, even as the many rubber shops that grew up in town were absorbed into the U.S. Rubber Company. "Along the west bank of the river stretching southward for a half-mile rose tiers of old tires and other junked rubber dumped in the yards of the regenerating plant," noted historian Constance Green. "Rubber workers' houses and tenements lined Rubber Avenue and the hillsides sloping down to Long Meadow Brook. The most casual visitor could scarcely fail to detect the dominance of rubber." Especially, it might be added, if that visitor had a nose to smell with.

But other companies grew up in town as well. In 1858, J.H. Whittemore and Howard B. Tuttle began the manufacture of malleable iron tools for use in farming and construction. The company would later be known as the Eastern Malleable Iron Company and it would produce metal for scores of different uses. The Risdon Company produced items that varied from safety pins to fuse sockets. Naugatuck Chemical produced heavy acids. The Peter Paul Company produced Mounds and Almond Joy candy bars.

The factories attracted workers from throughout the Northeast and certainly from overseas. Downtown Naugatuck and the various communities within its 16.2 square miles began to take on a distinctive ethnic diversity that continues to hold true today. The Union City part of town, for instance, was described in 1938 as "the foreign section of town. Polish weddings are often held in this area, where gay music crashes out from a rented hall."

The booming factories also brought a prosperity that was evidenced in many public and private buildings that were constructed around the turn of the century. Just as in Waterbury where members of the Chase family became admirers and patrons of the noted architect Cass Gilbert, so in Naugatuck did J.H. Whittemore become a devotee and friend of Sanford White, of the noted architectural firm McKim, Mead and White. Consequently, downtown Naugatuck stands today as an otherwise unassuming showcase for that firm's work, with the old high school, the library, the Congregational church, Salem Elementary School, and the railroad station serving as examples.

This proud heritage is nicely incorporated into the Naugatuck of today. Much of the housing stock is solid and mature, located in well established neighborhoods. Housing prices remain very much a bargain compared with prices elsewhere in Connecticut. The traditionally high standards of Naugatuck's work force are carried through today in the old-line manufacturers, in newer ones such as General

DataComm, and in the various firms that have found the location and cost of Naugatuck's new industrial park to be unbeatable. Certainly, Naugatuck stands to benefit greatly from the Shopco Mall currently in the early planning stages for placement just over the northern town line in Waterbury.

Once again, the fates of Naugatuck and Waterbury seem intertwined, this time on a decidedly upward course.

OXFORD

Oxford is the southernmost town in Greater Waterbury, and, as such, it offers many advantages. It lies within easy commuting distance to New Haven, Bridgeport, and the towns of eastern Fairfield County, and offers more open space and lower real estate prices

Molten malleable metal is produced at the Eastern Company's foundry in Naugatuck. Photo by Robert Houser

than most of the traditional suburbs in those areas.

Further, Oxford also offers superb inducements to commerce and industry. Most notable among these is the Waterbury-Oxford Airport, a state-operated, wholly modern, all-weather facility equipped to service private planes, executive jets, and freight carriers. In addition, from time to time, regularly scheduled commercial flights have gone in and out of Oxford.

Oxford is also proceeding with plans to encourage development by constructing a sewage line in its northern industrial zone. The zone is indicative of Oxford's many areas of potential. It comprises 3,000 acres, 750 of which are considered ideal for development. The town itself owns 127 acres within the zone that it plans to turn into an industrial park. The zone is very close to I-84 and it actually surrounds the airport. Its location relative to the southern and southwestern part of Connecticut certainly would seem to make it one of the great untapped areas for development in the entire western part of the state.

If the idea of locating in Oxford catches on, as it should, it would represent the first such general trend in more than 100 years. Oxford was first settled in 1678 by farmers moving out of Derby, and it largely remained a farming community through its incorporation in 1798 and in the years following. But during the eighteenth century Derby was a remarkably thriving city, and Oxford was able to benefit from that.

Derby was located at the head of the navigable portion of the Housatonic River. As such, in the early years of the colony, Derby conducted waterborne commerce with Boston, New York, the other colonies, and, most notably, the West Indies. Derby's port position inland relative to Bridgeport and New Haven was important at that time because transport over water was much cheaper and quicker than transport over the extremely rough roads of the day. As a consequence, it was not an uncommon sight in Derby in those days to find Derby Avenue lined with hundreds of wagons owned by Connecticut farmers and manufacturers waiting to load livestock and provisions onto the 100-ton vessels lined up at the Derby piers. The city's streets were also likely to be laden with hogsheads of rum, brandies, sugar, molasses, and fruits from the islands, as well as the fine manufactured goods of France, Spain, and Holland.

In all of this, a town like Oxford was able to play a modest role. Its farmers were able to readily market their grain, pork, butter, and cheese. In addition, small woolen mills and tanneries located in town were able to produce woolen and leather goods from Oxford sheep and cattle for export abroad. This manufacturing spirit expanded in Oxford to include such items as kegs and casks, hay rakes, hats, screws, shoes, and croquet sets. It continued on a small scale un-

A quiet day reading in the park makes a weekend special. Courtesy, Marantha Photo

til, first, Derby lost its advantage over New Haven and Bridgeport in the early 1800s, and, second, Oxford found itself bypassed by the railroads in the mid-1800s. From that time, Oxford's population dropped, and it did not really pick up again until after World War II when the town began to come into its own as a residential, regional suburb.

And so Oxford remains today, strategically located to take advantage of any movement away from the high costs and overcrowding of Fairfield County and other parts of southern Connecticut and New York. Its airport stands ready to serve all of western Connecticut, and its developable acres are minutes away from the interstate and from the IBM and Uniroyal complexes. It appears that Oxford is ideally suited to grow with the rest of the region.

PROSPECT

Prospect's main charms have always been residential, and they remain so today as the town has become home to a large number of single-family residences meant largely for those who earn their wages in Waterbury, New Haven, or elsewhere.

The roots of Prospect lie entirely in Waterbury and Cheshire, from which the town was incorporated in 1827. The ridge of rock that runs through Prospect on a north-south line was a natural boundary recognized by the Indians, by the settlers coming south from Hartford, Farmington, and Waterbury, and by the settlers coming north from New Haven, Wallingford, and Cheshire. The ridge also gave the town its name, the "prospect," or view, being "excelled nowhere in the county," according to a nineteenth century observer.

Prospect was originally known as Columbia. It was settled in its eastern section by those from Cheshire (who confused matters by referring to the section as West Rocks) and in the western, or Straitsville, section by Waterburians. Three chestnut trees, sometimes known as "Three Brothers" and sometimes as "Three Sisters," stood between the two main areas of town until they were felled by blight early in this century. In no part of town, however, were the prospects for farming great. "The general surface has a mountainous aspect," wrote a historian in the 1890s. "Huge boulders crop out on every hand, and although some of the lands have been tilled more than a hundred years, there are but a few fields that are free from stones. A limited area has productive soil, where some good crops are pro-

This Southbury School is a formidable institution. Photo by Jack McConnell

duced. Grazing and orchard products give occupation to many of the inhabitants . . ."

For wintertime fun take a sleigh ride in Southbury! Photo by Georgia Sheron

In light of this, it is not surprising to learn that Prospect enjoyed some early success in milling and manufacturing, and that for a while before it became a separate town it was even considered the most industrial section of Waterbury. During the early 1800s, Prospect joined the other towns in the region in producing a remarkable variety of goods, from Britannia ware to matches to suspender buckles to umbrella trimmings. It was in Prospect that Eben Tuttle first manufactured his highly regarded hoes, an activity he later removed to Naugatuck, where it grew into the enormous Eastern Malleable Iron Company. And eventually, most of the other manufacturers and small shops moved off to be near better power sources or better transportation.

And Prospect became, as it remains today, a quiet and pleasant place to buy or build a house and raise a family. And a popular place as well. In 1987, of all the towns in the region, only Water-

bury, Naugatuck, Watertown, and Cheshire (all far larger in population) built more new housing units than did Prospect. It appears
that its "in between" location is at last to its advantage. It remains
removed from the crowds of the cities, yet close enough for an early
commute. As a result, Prospect has never had it so good.

SOUTHBURY

The present-day dynamism of Greater Waterbury is best evidenced in
three fast-growing towns on three different sides of Waterbury: Cheshire to the east, Watertown to the north, and Southbury to the
west. In many respects, Southbury's recent growth and change have
been the most intense, almost entirely due to the new million-square-
foot IBM installation near the intersection of Route 6 and I-84. Yet
this enormous addition to the landscape is really only the latest in a series of changes that have marked Southbury's gradual transformation
from a small farming community.

Southbury has been evolving for some time now. Its location in between Waterbury and Danbury, its four interchanges with I-84, and
its 40 lovely square miles have proved irresistible to those searching
for homes or for business locations. Most of Southbury today still ex-
udes a country charm. There is peace to be found in its pastures, its
country crossroads, or in any one of its four state parks. But where development has been allowed, it has flourished—most recently with
IBM, with the Jordan Marsh-anchored Southbury Plaza, and with the
new Ramada Renaissance Hotel.

Southbury was first settled in 1673, as part of Pomperaug (later
Woodbury), by dissidents from Stratford who had left their parish in
search of fertile land to the north. Southbury was long considered a self-
contained village, but it was not incorporated by the General Assembly until 1787. For many years, its main pursuits were agricultural,
but the waterpower of the Pomperaug River and the busy Main
Street each contributed a fair share of commerce to Southbury's fortunes. In 1854, for instance, a historian noted that

*Southbury now constitutes a beautiful, fertile farming town, well wa-
tered by the Pomperaug River, its branches, and other streams . . .
There are in the town three taverns, four blacksmith shops, several
shoe shops, one saddler's shop, four grist mills, ten saw mills, one
paper mill, one manufactory for edge tools, several wool hat manufac-
tories, one satinet manufactory . . . and seven stores.*

By the end of the nineteenth century, much of the intense manufacturing activity—especially in the South Britain part of town—had
relocated to the larger cities. Southbury was described in 1892:
"Agriculture is the chief pursuit of the town, whose population has

in consequence decreased, being attracted to manufacturing centers." And not much had evidently changed by 1938, when yet another observer remarked that "an air of quiet and comfort pervades the village. Residents sell their land only after careful consideration of the qualifications of the buyers."

And such could still be described as the case today. The development in Southbury over the past 20 years or so has been contained and carefully considered. Yet in large part it has benefited the entire region.

It all began with the construction of the interstate in the 1960s. This was followed shortly thereafter by a major development in Southbury's fortunes—the construction of Heritage Village, the nationally recognized and acclaimed adult residential complex. Heritage Village not only brought several thousand new residents into town virtually overnight, but it also created a demand for the stores, restaurants, hotels, and other services that soon were to follow—most notably at the Harrison Inn and other establishments right at the Village.

Today, with Heritage Village quite thoroughly absorbed into and a part of the community, IBM, with its 2,500 employees, presents the latest formidable challenge. Already, the town, and especially the area around the complex itself, is evolving yet again. But Southbury's ability to absorb change while retaining its essential character is well established. There is little doubt but that it will be able to do so again.

THOMASTON

It is not often that the efforts of one person so influence the development, the character, and even the name of a community as Seth Thomas's efforts influenced Thomaston. But the town's reputation as a small but able manufacturing community with skilled workers is a direct link back to its days as a prodigious producer of clocks.

For the first hundred years or so after its earliest settlement, Plymouth Hollow (the future Thomaston) enjoyed unexceptional circumstances. Located along the Naugatuck River and far removed physically from the rest of the Town of Plymouth, the community scratched out a living from whatever farming or small manufacturing could be devised. In fact, in all of Plymouth Hollow at the beginning of the 1800s there were perhaps a dozen dwellings, according to a historian of the time.

But then Seth Thomas came to town in 1812. Born in Wolcott in 1785, Thomas, after meager education and a brief apprenticeship, had gone into the clock business as a carpenter with Eli Terry and Silas Hoadley in 1809 in what would later be known as the Terryville section of Plymouth. After one year, Terry sold his interest in the company to Thomas and Hoadley. After two more years, Thomas left Hoadley and went down the hill and across the river to Plymouth Hollow, where he first manufactured grandfather clocks, and then, for $1,000, bought the rights to the shelf clock developed by Terry.

The clock, as manufactured by Seth Thomas, sold for $5, instead of the $25 that had been common. As clock sales took off, the factory and the town around it boomed. As a contemporary noted, "The quiet little hamlet . . . has grown to one of the loveliest manufacturing towns in Connecticut."

Seth Thomas' moves over the ensuing years continued to benefit the townspeople. He built a cotton mill in 1834. He persuaded the railroad in the 1840s to get from Waterbury to Winsted through Plymouth Hollow rather than through Watertown. Later, he was angered that the town fathers of Waterbury had allowed a competing clock factory to set up shop in that city, so he vowed to buy no more Waterbury brass. Instead, in 1853, he built his own brass mill, later (and today) known as Plume and Atwood.

And through it all, Seth Thomas built houses for his workers all along the main streets of the town, which gradually became

Seth Thomas began making clocks in Thomaston; this renovated Seth Thomas factory building houses 16 different companies and 300 employees. Photo by Georgia Sheron

known as "Thomas Town," and when it was incorporated in 1875, as Thomaston.

Today, Thomaston remains a manufacturing town, with many of its 6,700 residents working in small machine shops. The huge Seth Thomas plant was finally abandoned by the company as it moved south in 1982. Recently, however, new life has come to the old plant in the form of an industrial commons, where 16 widely differing firms currently employ 300 persons—an innovative use of the old space that no doubt would make Seth Thomas proud.

Thomaston's location is also very much in favor these days. It is

Watertown High School is proud of its baseball team. Photo by Georgia Sheron

located squarely on the Route 8 corridor that runs north of Waterbury and is widely regarded as a very likely path of industrial and commercial development in the coming decade. At the same time, Thomaston is now a popular residential town as well, due first to its stock of affordable older houses, but also because it can claim several desirable Litchfield hills for its own, and they are suddenly sprouting an impressive array of decidedly upscale houses.

Thomaston has nicely weathered the economic wars common to the towns of the Naugatuck Valley. Its solid industrial base has adapted and diversified. Its history as a small, self-contained city—its strong family values and local enthusiasm—has blended well with its later-day role as a suburb.

WATERTOWN

Perhaps better than any other town in the region, Watertown represents all of the advantages of life in Greater Waterbury. Although it is growing and changing rapidly, Watertown demonstrates diverse strengths. Its location is superb, its manufacturing and commercial bases are well established and significant, yet it contains much of the feel of Litchfield County and is much sought-after as a place in which to live.

Watertown is neatly divided by U.S. Route 6. To the north of this line are the farms, parks, lakes, and woodlands that make up much of Litchfield County and much of traditional New England. To the south are some farms, but also Watertown's commercial downtown, the heavily residential Oakville section, and most of the town's business and industry.

There are over 50 manufacturers located in Watertown. Many are small metalworking shops that use the skilled workers the area is known for. Local companies like Heminway and Bartlett, Bristol Babcock, and Siemon Corporation rub shoulders with divisions of GTE, Litton, and P.F. Kaufman. In addition, Watertown's uncrowded access to Route 8 and five minutes' distance from I-84 has recently made it the location for Roadway Express and UPS terminals, and for the distribution of Crystal Rock bottled water, which moved from Stamford in 1988.

Watertown enjoys an interesting and varied history. The threat of Indian attack kept the very early settlers away until about 1700, when Obadiah Richards moved in. By 1738, the first church society had been established under the name of Westbury, although separation from Waterbury was not completed until 1780. Many of Watertown's earliest achievements were agricultural. It was in Watertown, for instance, that David Humphreys successfully bred the first Spanish merino sheep, providing superior wool for his mill and superior garments for all of America. It was also from Watertown that the famous Connecticut Red draft cattle originated.

It was agriculture that was behind some of Watertown's most memorable days, particularly those associated with James Bishop, proprietor of Bishop's Tavern during the mid-1800s and one of the great self-promoters of that or any other time. One of Bishop's annual stunts was the haying of his entire 50-acre meadow in one day. To do this he gathered men and boys from all over Watertown in his field, and he invited all interested townspeople to view the event. Following the blast of a horn at sunrise, everyone went to work. Bishop provided five meals and plenty of switchel and rum,

A patchwork of farmland creates a crazy quilt of prosperity. Photo by Georgia Sheron

and the enormous task was invariably completed in time.

One year, Bishop went a step further and announced that the entire load of hay would be piled onto a single wagon and transported to New Haven. He then had a huge wagon specially built, and he had trees cut back, tollgates removed, and bridges widened all along what today is Route 63 to New Haven. When the great day came, the wagon was pulled by 12 pairs of fine Devon oxen, their yokes bedecked with scarlet streamers. On top of the hay sat a small band that played lively tunes while Bishop traveled in an accompanying barouche, accepting the accolades of the crowd that lined the route.

But Watertown's history is also steeped in manufacturing. It was home to the first American factory to spool silk and the first to make pins; it was an early manufacturer of buttons. Later, Watertown produced items as varied as bull rings ("of superior strength and quality"), palm leaf hats, mousetraps, and Watertown Wool Dusters.

In 1938, Watertown was described as "another one of Connecticut's 'parlor towns'." This was an unfair assessment, although it probably refers to the town's lovely and genteel central residential area, which features a number of fine neighborhoods and homes. Included in this part of town—and an important part of the community as a whole—is Taft School, which came to Watertown in 1893 after its founding in Pelham Manor, New York, in 1890. Taft is one of the leading preparatory schools in the nation; its campus, its facilities, and its many events provide the town with a critical resource.

Today's Watertown is a dynamic place. Its housing stock, both of single-family houses and condominiums, is growing rapidly. Its recent accommodations for business and industrial expansion—such as the 135-acre Heritage Technology Park or the Siemon Company's Princeton Center with its shared-technology set-up—show that Watertown is intent upon remaining a key part of the region's rebirth.

WOLCOTT

Those who have not been to Wolcott in the last ten years or so will be surprised to see how the town has grown. Although it remains largely suburban in nature, with an excellent stock of modest single-family homes, Wolcott is now also growing with newly constructed luxury homes and a good deal of retail and commercial activity along its principal roads.

Wolcott sits along the very top of the Metacomet Ridge, known locally as Southington Mountain. From the top of the ridge, one is allowed a spectacular eastward view, which is probably why the Tunxis Indians chose the spot for one of their lodges—and why first settler Thomas Judd built his cabin there in 1690.

For many years after its settlement, Wolcott remained a quiet community. There were several mills in operation along the Mad River, Roar-

Downtown Woodbury appears to be a tiny village among the trees in this aerial photo. Photo by Jack McConnell

ing Brook, and Old Tannery Brook, but most of the residents did what farming could be done along the town's rocky hills. In fact, it could even be said that manufacturing was not encouraged. Around 1812, Wolcott native Seth Thomas (who had been derided as "Dan Tuttle's fool" around town during his apprenticeship to a carpenter) agreed to purchase a mill along the Mad River if the town fathers would agree to improve the road that ran from Wolcott to Cheshire—the quickest way to New Haven. The town fathers, however, must not have seen much of a future in Seth Thomas clocks. They refused to improve the road and Thomas went off to Plymouth Hollow, where his clockmaking was such a success that the community changed its name to Thomaston.

The story of how Wolcott got its name is an interesting one as well. The community was known as Farmingbury in 1796 when it

Antiquing is a rich adventure in Woodbury's shops. Photo by Jack McConnell

sought to break away from Waterbury and incorporate on its own. When the vote came in on the petition at the state General Assembly, it was a tie, and the tie had to be broken by Lieutenant Governor Oliver Wolcott. Wolcott cast his vote in favor of incorporation, and the grateful residents named their new town in his honor.

Wolcott, however, lost population throughout the nineteenth century as farmers gave up scrambling along the hills and moved west, and as other workers moved closer to the new factories in Waterbury and elsewhere. By 1870, Wolcott was the third-smallest town in the state. By 1920, Arthur Baker would write a poem in which the early glory days of the town were recalled and the present-day lamented:

When George Washington was still a little boy
The folks who lived where Waterbury stands
Bought goods in Wolcott; filled their powder horns
Got lead to mold their bullets. But today
a bag of peanuts or a spool of thread
could not be had for love and money both.

However, the poem goes on to predict that:

Someday soon
Those hills will be repeopled with a race
Who've farmed the slopes of Italy or Greece . . .

And that has certainly turned out to be the case. As Waterbury expanded and its citizens sought space in the neighboring hills, Wolcott was rediscovered, primarily as a residential suburb. Today, Wolcott is a town of more than 14,000 persons. Its nearness to Waterbury and even Hartford makes it largely a bedroom community, although some opportunities for development exist along the two main arteries of Wolcott Road and Meriden Road.

WOODBURY

The museum villages of Old Sturbridge, Massachusetts, and Williamsburg, Virginia, are attempts to recreate that which still exists in Woodbury. The town is a living museum of American architectural styles from the seventeenth century to almost yesterday. In Woodbury real people live and work and play in some 300 years of historic houses, commercial, religious and governmental buildings and surrounding landscape. Superb Georgian, Federal, Greek Revival, Gothic Revival, Italianate, Stick Style, Neoclassical Revival, and a veritable textbook of other Victorian and twentieth-century styles coexist— sometimes side by side, sometimes across the street from each other, sometimes isolated from neighbors by expanses of landscape. Change has come slowly and carefully to Woodbury and has respected both the past and the landscape. It is this quality of completeness . . . that gives the town such importance.

So was Woodbury described in 1975 for a historical survey of the town, and so it remains today—a lovely New England country town where history is in evidence around every corner.

Woodbury is older than Waterbury. It was settled in 1673, when 15 families broke away from their church in Stratford and headed north into the very agreeable Pomperaug Valley. As they settled into the fertile region—and as others soon followed—the new community represented the western frontier of America, with no other white settlement between the Pomperaug and the Pacific Ocean.

Woodbury turned out to be, as it was described by the Pootatuck Indians during their deed negotiations with the first settlers, "a goodly place for many smokes of the white man." Although much of the original town was pieced off, what remained was the best farming land in the region, "a calcareous loam, warm and fertile, well adapted to the production of corn and the various kinds of grain." Although Woodbury briefly fell under the spell of the manufacturing

boom of the mid-1800s (producing cashmere shawls, cutlery, watches, and the inevitable buttons), it soon reverted back to farming, and it retains a mostly rural bearing today.

Woodbury's Main Street and its center are nearly as pleasant today as it must have been in 1854, when local historian William Cothren wrote, "The central village is pleasantly situated in a level and extended valley on the Pomperaug . . . it is surrounded on every side by high hills, forming a kind of amphitheater. Beautiful walks and drives abound in every direction." Today, the southern part of

Red barns dot the countryside of Woodbury. Photo by Jack McConnell

town along Route 6 is home to some commercial growth of a rather modest nature, but the center of town is quite charming (a number of the original residences are now occupied by antique shops).

Woodbury's countryside and its wonderful houses are much sought after these days. Some of the houses are used as weekend retreats for harried New Yorkers, while others have long been used by writers and artists who seek a rural setting that is still within earshot of big city publishers and galleries. As a whole, Woodbury is a critical element of the appeal of the whole Waterbury region.

Photo by Jack McConnell

Epilogue

Picture Greater Waterbury in the year 2000. Waterbury itself will have fully reclaimed its role as a leading city in Connecticut, crackling with vitality and change. The gritty and dark old capital of heavy industry will have been transformed into the hub of one of the busiest white-collar areas in the Northeast. As new jobs spring up in Southbury and Watertown and Cheshire, Waterbury will once again serve as the heart and muscle of the region, providing goods and services and hard, skilled labor to the suburbs.

The region's manufacturing base will remain stable, as it continues to diversify and shift according to the dictates of the global marketplace. As Connecticut competes economically with other countries, rather than other states, in order to sell its goods and services, Waterbury will be a part of that story. Entrepreneurs and fledgling businesses will continue to come to the area for the low costs and the skills of the work force—and they'll stay because they like the way of life. The Naugatuck Valley will continue to hum with machinery and new ideas.

Waterbury's skillfully refurbished and rebuilt downtown will continue to thrive. Between now and the end of the century, it will be discovered as an economical and strategically correct location for office space—away from the overtaxed roads and nonexistent parking elsewhere, yet close to all it needs to be close to. Office space will be available in the many wonderful old buildings that exist in Waterbury, but new buildings will go up as well. For there is still room to grow in Waterbury, still room for a vision to take shape and substance. The city's 28.8 square miles compare favorably to Hartford's 18.4 square miles, Bridgeport's 17.5, and New Haven's 21.1. This elbow room in Waterbury will become more and more of an advantage as the years go by. Indeed, office space will be available all along I-84, especially in Southbury, where the full effect of IBM will be played out, and in Cheshire, where the business and commercial parks will be tenanted and busy.

The main growth, however, in the intermediate future will likely take place up the Route 8 corridor, through Watertown, Thomaston, and beyond. The restless waves of commerce, now moving up from Greater New York and backing down from Hartford, will meet in Waterbury and then surge north, where roads are already built, costs are very low, industrial parks are waiting, and life is pleasantly uncomplicated.

Such a trend would further enhance Waterbury's position as a hub: as the center for distribution and transportation; for banking, legal, and other services; for government functions; and even, eventually, for entertainment and culture.

Much of the region will also continue to be a source of moderately priced housing, both in new houses and condominiums as well as in older housing stock. The neighborhood ethic—and the pride it engenders—will remain firm. Those who look ahead project that Waterbury and the immediate area will remain socially stable for many years to come and that it is far more able to withstand storms in the economy than it was 20 years ago.

Finally, the many projects now on the drawing boards or under construction will have been completed, adding a good deal of luster to an already brightening scene.

A big, new hotel, a new office building on the Green, and a magnificently restored old theater will bring glamour and a nighttime scene to downtown Waterbury. New retail malls, possibly in Waterbury, Watertown, or Cheshire, will keep retail spending largely within the region. Further corporate activity is likely, especially in the hills of Southbury, Middlebury, and Oxford, where large tracts of land already are held by Fortune 500 firms.

But through it all, there is little doubt that Waterbury will remain Waterbury.

It will remain a place in which a large and productive middle class provides a stability often lacking in other cities where wealth and poverty are at odds with one another.

It will remain a city and region whose people welcome new things but who do not cling to the latest fad or fashion.

It will remain a place that has made its own way in the world, whose successes were earned through an ability to think and work hard, rather than through the good luck of geographical location or proximity to a sellable natural resource.

Waterburians, and those throughout region, are a stubborn bunch. They are secure in their place among the hills and the valleys. They have survived Indian attacks, the floods and plagues of the seventeenth century, the fire of 1902, the flood of 1955, the abandonment by the brass industry. And as they've survived, they've learned—and Waterbury has emerged as strong as it's ever been. It has kept what was important from the old as it accepts what looks to be lasting from the new. It has emerged from its long night with its integrity intact, with its strengths undiminished, and with its soul gloriously alive. It is ready to be recognized once again as a great American city.

Green fields and a little red barn create a picture-perfect scene of rural Waterbury. Photo by Jack McConnell

A Region's Enterprises

Photo by Georgia Sheron

Networks

Waterbury's energy, communication, and transportation providers keep products, information, and power circulating inside and outside the area.

The Waterbury Republican and American, 146

Northeast Utilities, 147

General DataComm Industries, 148

Unisys, 150

WTXX-TV Channel 20, 152

Courtesy, Waterbury Convention and Visitors Commission

THE WATERBURY REPUBLICAN AND AMERICAN

The Waterbury Republican *and* American, *run by the Pape family since 1901, are among the few remaining locally owned dailies in Connecticut. The newspapers are housed in the city's former railroad station, built in 1908, a building well known for its magnificent clock tower.*

Growing with the community they serve, the morning *Waterbury Republican* and afternoon *American* newspapers reflect greater Waterbury's dynamic evolution while respecting its heritage and the family values of its residents.

These are among the few remaining locally owned daily newspapers in Connecticut. All decisions regarding news coverage and business practices are made in Waterbury with the best long-term interests of the community and its citizens in mind.

The newspapers' publisher, William J. Pape II, today sustains a reputation for vigorous, independent coverage of local news begun by his grandfather, W.J. Pape, in 1901. For their courageous exposure of graft in City Hall, the newspapers earned a Pulitzer Gold Medal in 1939.

When the first edition of the *Waterbury American* was published in 1844, there were no head-

lines and very little local news for the city's 3,000 residents to read. A poem entitled "Complaint of the Poor" by Robert Southey dominated an upper corner, and the four-page newspaper was filled with philosophical essays.

The newspaper soon evolved to become a strong and steadfast mirror of the community.

A sister newspaper, the *Waterbury Republican,* which publishes a Sunday edition called the *Sunday Republican,* was established in 1881 as a morning paper.

Today the newspapers remain the only Connecticut newspapers to have been awarded the Pulitzer Gold Medal for Meritorious Public Service.

Local ownership makes for local emphasis. In an era of media conglomerates where publishers' offices are often hundreds of miles away, the Waterbury papers give a refreshing, involved outlook, providing local coverage by people who

know, understand, and often live in the communities they cover.

The Waterbury newspapers take their responsibility to the community seriously. They sponsor a Newspaper in Education Program that is accredited by the Connecticut Board of Education.

The Campership Fund is another program the newspaper sponsors, raising from $30,000 to $40,000 each year to provide some 400 underprivileged youngsters with the opportunity to attend camp.

The Waterbury newspapers are housed in the landmark Union Station building, a gracious red-brick edifice built by the New Haven Railroad in 1909 for $332,000. At the time roughly 86 trains would pass through Waterbury each day. The building was purchased by the *Waterbury Republican* and *American* in 1952, and opened as a newspaper office six years later, after considerable renovations, including the addition of a second floor inside the massive waiting room.

The building incorporates one of the larger clock towers in New England. At 240 feet high, the tower is modeled after the Torre de Mangia on the Palazzo Publico in Sienna, Italy.

In that building, through the use of sophisticated computer systems and modern printing equipment, 41,000 copies of the *Republican* are printed each morning and 26,000 of the *American* each afternoon. On Sundays the circulation increases above 74,000.

The *Waterbury Republican* and *American,* and the *Sunday Republican* keep readers throughout northwestern Connecticut fully informed on hometown happenings and international events.

NORTHEAST UTILITIES

Thomas Edison's famous incandescent lamp experiments opened the doors to a new industry that was to revolutionize America. Just 14 months after he put his theory into practice, establishing the nation's first electric lighting plant at the historic Pearl Street Station in New York City in 1882, a company was organized to utilize electricity for lighting in Waterbury.

This marked the beginning of a new era of growth and development in the Brass City. The firm was named The Connecticut District Telegraph and Electric Company, which remains somewhat of a puzzle since there was no district telegraph in Waterbury at the time. Later the name was changed to the Connecticut Electric Company.

The new enterprise established its first plant in a frame building on the grounds of the Waterbury Farrell Foundry and Machine Company, and in June 1885 onlookers were mesmerized as the city's first 30 streetlamps were lit. Five years later the firm built a brick station on Freight Street that had a capacity of 970 kilowatts. By 1894 its electricity powered about 175 arc lights in Waterbury stores and mills, about 7,000 incandescent lights in stores and homes, and 175 streetlights.

Through the years the company has evolved, changing name and ownership several times and completing its metamorphosis in 1917 as The Connecticut Light and Power Company (CL&P). Today CL&P is the principal subsidiary of the Northeast Utilities (NU) system, which has served approximately 1.4 million electric and gas customers in Connecticut and western Massachusetts.

From the age of streetlights to the era of strobe lights, electric service has expanded considerably in its first 105 years. CL&P and the entire NU system look to a future of further growth and change.

To strengthen its responsiveness to the needs of its customers

and provide energy for a growing economy, NU has developed a wide-ranging series of resources, including energy conservation and the use of nuclear energy, oil, natural gas, coal, hydropower, cogeneration, and small power production.

To extend its leadership in an increasingly competitive energy marketplace, NU has begun implementing an ambitious, four-part business plan. This includes expansion of its electric business, exploration of new energy-related business opportunities, divestiture of CL&P's gas business, and a competitive strategy based on improved customer service, cost management, and a schedule of rates that more accurately reflects the true costs of providing service to each group of customers.

In keeping with NU's strong commitment to the communities it

Energy-efficient technologies can make the difference between life and death for energy-intensive industries. The Plume and Atwood Brass Mill in Thomaston replaced an outdated and inefficient static casting process with a modern continuous casting process, thus realizing very significant cost savings. Richard S. Zampiello (left), president of Plume and Atwood, tells NU Energy Management Services senior consultant James C. Allen how the new technology lowered production costs.

serves, employees contribute their time, energy, and personal resources to many civic, charitable, and community service organizations. NU is determined to continue as a strong and effective partner in the economic development of the greater Waterbury area and the rest of New England by ensuring the safe, reliable, and cost-effective delivery of electricity and related services.

GENERAL DATACOMM INDUSTRIES

From street to street, city to city, continent to continent, the transmission of information proceeds at a rate that approaches the fantastic. And as the information explosion puts a world of data at our fingertips, General DataComm Industries serves as a key player, a leading supplier of advanced systems and products that allow organizations to build and manage communication networks that transmit data, voice, and video over private and public telecommunications facilities.

its U.S. and Canadian reservation systems through a modem network hubbed in New York. An influential Far Eastern newspaper gathers data and transmits information over a network link connecting its major printing and distribution centers in Tokyo, Los Angeles, and New York. Telemetry data is transmitted by GDC equipment for the space shuttle in applications requiring extremely high reliability. High-speed multiplexers and unique data-over-voice products were uti-

ABOVE: All GDC products undergo rigorous testing to meet requirements for functionality, reliability, and quality assurance.

LEFT: Corporate headquarters for General DataComm Industries is in the Middlebury countryside, a town just west of Waterbury.

On the frontier of technology, General DataComm has been a pioneer in the field since its founding in 1969. Since then the company has developed one of the broadest lines of transmission products in the communications industry. These include products and systems referred to as multiplexers, modems, data sets, and network control and diagnostic devices.

GDC products are in use worldwide. A major U.S. bank, for example, transmits data routinely between Hong Kong, Tokyo, London, and New York using a GDC network. A European airline monitors

lized by a local telephone company in creating a data-transmission system established over existing telephone lines for the U.S. Army.

With the help of General Data-Comm's expertise in global networking, it is indeed becoming a small world for the company's domestic and international customers, which include small and large corporations, government agencies, multinationals, domestic Bell operating companies, and other major common carriers worldwide.

Whatever the product or system, GDC operates with the same philosophy it has had since its incep-

tion: develop and install communication systems that allow organizations to transmit information nationwide or around the world, provide the best systems or products possible, and sustain all customers with outstanding service and support. These objectives are realized through a comprehensive business strategy that represents a fusion of technology, products, people, and facilities into a single integrated market thrust.

In satisfying customer requirements, GDC representatives first meet with clients to determine communication needs and assess the system environment at the customer site. Subsequently, the system is designed and installation plans estab-

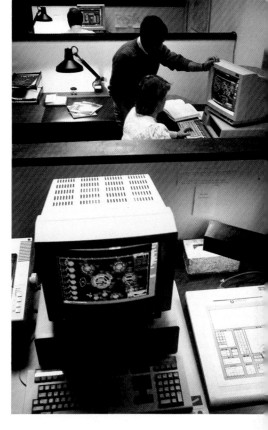

lished.

Product quality is a critical commitment at General DataComm—from conception through design, manufacturing, and installation. Once a system is installed, customers are assured that their ongoing requirements for service and support will be met by the comprehensive capabilities that GDC provides.

In a highly competitive, leading-edge industry, success requires an in-depth knowledge of the market, a focused marketing position, responsive engineering, and strong manufacturing capabilities. GDC's funding of research and development efforts assures steady progression of new technologies and products to serve the needs of the marketplace. The company aggressively seeks better solutions to information transmission by developing equipment and systems directed at fast growing segments of the marketplace. This operating philosophy has made it one of the leaders in a sophisticated industry.

Today's technology is creating high expectations, and customers—having absorbed yesterday's advances—are constantly seeking new levels of performance and capabilities. In an environment where silicon technology is basic to the design of virtually every electronic product, innovation proceeds at a

ABOVE: Advanced assembly techniques are used at the Naugatuck facility. Ribbons of individual electronic components are assembled for specific production runs.

RIGHT: Assisted by computer-aided design (CAD) technology, system design specialists at GDC are involved with customers as consultants and designers on a wide range of information networks that respond to specific business needs and applications.

rapid pace. Facilitated by the incorporation of complex hardware and comprehensive software, the industry is driving toward faster speeds, more functionality, increased flexibility, and greater efficiency. In addition, the merger of communications and computer technologies has created a high level of interrelationship, further accelerating the pace of activity.

As with all companies, GDC employees are unquestionably one of the firm's most important assets—from research to design to manufacturing to sales and support. To increase employee participation in all facets of the business, GDC has developed an Employee Involvement Program based on quality circle methods. Employees with different business skills and corporate assignments are organized into teams to analyze and address a broad spectrum of challenges and opportunities for improvement,

and to recommend a course of action.

The company employs approximately 2,300 employees worldwide, including 1,800 at its headquarters locations in Connecticut. GDC has major subsidiaries in Canada and in the United Kingdom, and maintains a network of sales offices throughout North America, Europe, the Far East, and Australia.

Locally the company is involved in a variety of activities, including membership in community organizations and the United Way, scholarship programs to area colleges, and Partners in Education, a program cosponsored by the Greater Waterbury Area Chamber of Commerce, Connecticut Light and Power, and the Waterbury School System.

Whether in the Waterbury area or on the international front, whether working with employees or sophisticated networks, General DataComm Industries is playing its part in bringing the world closer together.

UNISYS

When the war effort was at its peak in the early 1940s, Wheeler Insulated Wire was hard at work, playing its part as a supplier of enamel wire. The company, which subsequently underwent several name changes, today operates as Unisys, part of the $10-billion Unisys Corporation, and is still involved in the defense industry.

The company has evolved through the years, always with its feet firmly planted in the present and with an eye toward the future, incorporating change as part of its strategy of long-range planning. Unisys has traditionally been on the leading edge of the defense industry and continues in that position, with its Waterbury facility providing components and subassemblies for such important systems as radar antennae and shipboard radar.

The 100,000-square-foot Waterbury facility is part of the parent company's Defense Systems operation. The Waterbury facility is largely devoted to the assembly and test of components and subsystems used in radar and weapons systems. Today this primarily consists of the assembly of wire harnesses, circuit card assemblers, cable, chassis, and cabinets.

What is now the Waterbury facility began in 1909, when it was founded as the Wheeler Insulated Wire Company. When it was purchased in 1943 by the Sperry Gyroscope Company, it became part of a major defense firm. It continued to grow in a key role as a manufacturing facility for Sperry, and when the Sperry and Burroughs corporations merged in 1986 to form Unisys, the Waterbury facility continued its key functions. The plant is now a part of the corporation's Shipboard and Ground Systems Group, headquartered in Great Neck, New York, the largest single group within Unisys Defense Systems. The Great Neck facility performs much of the design, procure-

The Waterbury plant has been completely refurbished to provide both an attractive working environment and compliance with all military environmental specifications. The innovative use of automated storage and retrieval equipment allows the company to devote 75,000 square feet directly to manufacturing.

ment, marketing, and other activities that involve the Waterbury facility's products.

There are about 500 workers at the Waterbury facility—employees who have ample opportunity to leave their mark on the nation's defense system. The firm has produced subsystems, for example, for the AEGIS Ship Combat System, one of the most advanced systems now employed by the United States Navy. It has also produced parts for the U.S. Navy Terrier and Harpoon Missile and Control System.

Through the years the firm's products have become increasingly

ABOVE: *This Diamond transport system in the circuit card assembly area serves as a schedule and tracking system in addition to delivering work to the assembly operators. Bar coding allows Unisys to maintain real-time status on hundreds of part numbers and provides the capability of assembling all programs simultaneously.*

BELOW: *This MK 92 Servo Cabinet is a good example of the complex harness assembly and installation that is part of everyday life at the Unisys Waterbury plant. The subassembly harnesses must fit perfectly in the confined space of the cabinet..*

sophisticated. The level of skill required on the assembly floor has shifted from the most basic, involving a minimum of training, to the higher level of expertise required for the testing and integration of systems.

In 1950, for example, the firm was primarily concerned with producing transformers and chokes, including enamel wire, harnesses, and telephone components. In the 1960s the emphasis was on producing high-reliability transformers and chokes, including cordwood modules, circuit cards, harnesses, and rotary components.

The next decade saw the advent of the firm's specialization in

the area of refurbishing, primarily of electronic cabinets, including chassis, circuit cards, and harnesses. In the 1980s Unisys began not only to refurbish but also to assemble the cabinets. In the 1990s the trend is expected to be toward more sophisticated integration and testing.

This evolution is indicative of the firm's progressive approach and continuing commitment to providing the highest level of product and quality. Its long-term mission is to establish the capabilities to become the prime system manufacturing, test integration facility, as well as continuing its current role of providing cost-effective, high-quality, on-time support for Unisys Corporation's Great Neck facility.

The Waterbury facility maintains the highest of standards in accomplishing such goals. Excellence in all of its activities, coupled with personal and business integrity, is the cornerstone of the Unisys Defense Systems business posture in the marketplace.

The Aegis Director Assembly area highlights Waterbury's skill in assembling large electromechanical structures. Precision alignment in all phases of assembly is the key to this multi-ton radar's ability to quickly and accurately track its targets.

WTXX CHANNEL 20

When many Connecticut residents go to see a movie, they head not to the local cinema, but straight to their own television sets, turning the dial to Channel 20 WTXX, Connecticut's number-one movie station.

In addition to world television premier and contemporary and classic movies, the station offers a wide variety of other programming that has captured a strong market share of Connecticut viewers. In the course of a week, some 731,000 viewers will tune into Channel 20.

In April 1982 Channel 20 became the first independent television station in what is geographically known as the Hartford-New Haven television market, the 23rd-largest market in the country. At that time the Hartford-New Haven market was the largest in the country's more than 200 television markets that did not have an independent station. Previously Channel 20 was an NBC affiliate, but the station's owners wanted to offer an alternative to network programming.

The first major emphasis was on carving its niche for the movie viewer. The station currently has a collection surpassing 2,000 titles and often shows movies in week-long thematic presentations. The station's strongest audience is found in its movie programming, with Channel 20 providing more than 40 hours of movie viewing each week.

In addition to Channel 20's emphasis on movies, it has captured the hearts and funny bones of area viewers with daily showings of the all-time popular "M*A*S*H" series. This is indeed the entertainment staple of the station, drawing in devotees of those zany Korean War medicos.

Another focus is on live sports programming. The station covers both New York Mets baseball and Knicks basketball games.

And while Channel 20 does not offer newscasts, it does have a solid public affairs program, including "Insight Out," a weekly program that deals with local, regional, and statewide issues. Whenever possible it focuses on the greater Waterbury area, hammering home thought-provoking issues. The station also spotlights, through its public affairs spots, many community programs. It has aired telethons for the United Negro College Fund, the March of Dimes, and Easter Seals.

Channel 20 has achieved a mix of programming that it believes attracts its market audience, of which, studies show, typical viewers tend to be young and upscale adults between the ages of 18 and 54. A secondary market is children, attracted by the station's diversified and creative shows, which includes a puppet host, TX, who stimulates children's creativity through daily "Art and Riddles" sent in by viewers.

Channel 20 broadcasts from a state-of-the-art studio in Prospect, utilizing transmitting and produc-

tion equipment that is among the finest in the state. When the company was acquired in 1983 by Odyssey, its new owners invested more than $4 million in equipment, including a 1,000-foot tower and a supplemental 250-foot tower, both in Prospect.

The station's administrative offices are headquartered on Meadow Street, on the first floor of what once was the Anaconda building. While Channel 20 was the first Connecticut independent station, it has also been able to maintain its position as the leading adult independent with the entry of a second independent station in the market area.

Though just a short time ago Connecticut had only network affiliates in operation, independent television has clearly marked its territory in the Nutmeg State. Independents constitute one of the fastest growing markets in the country, and the business climate in Connecticut fosters a bright outlook for the continued progress of Channel 20.

According to viewing results determined by metering television sets, the independent audience has increased significantly in recent years as the network audience has declined, thus manifesting an obvious dissatisfaction with network programming, particularly in the past six or seven years.

Still, it is an extremely competitive climate. With its proximity to both New York and Boston, the Hartford-New Haven television market is considered among the

FACING PAGE: Channel 20 provides more than 40 hours of movie viewing each week, often in week-long thematic programming utilizing more than 2,000 titles.

THIS PAGE: The station broadcasts from a state-of-the-art studio in Prospect with transmitting and production equipment that is among the finest in the state.

most competitive in the country. There is also competition from the home video and cable television industries. Cable penetration, for example, had already reached 78 percent of the market in 1988, one of the highest levels in the country.

While cable penetration has increased over the years, Channel 20 has likewise increased its audience, a credit to the station's strong programming and promotional efforts. Channel 20 has launched a promotional campaign to get the message across about its unique breed of programming.

Channel 20 continues to increase its market share, attracting audiences with its vast repertoire of movies, its innovative and creative children's programming, its emphasis on sports, and its strong commitment to community service.

From its start as an independent station in 1982, Channel 20 has risen in status from the new kid on the block to a blockbusting success.

Manufacturing

Producing goods for individuals and industry, manufacturing firms provide employment for many Waterbury area residents.

Hubbard-Hall Inc., 156

Anamet Inc., 158

MacDermid Incorporated, 160

Airpax Corporation, 162

Lewis Electronic Instrumentation Division/Colt, 164

American Chemical & Refining Co., Inc., 165

The Siemon Company, 166

The Platt Brothers & Co., 168

Summit Corporation of America, 170

Risdon Corporation, 172

The Eastern Company, 173

Truelove & Maclean Inc., 174

Bristol Babcock Inc., 175

Timex, 176

Photo by Georgia Sheron

HUBBARD-HALL INC.

Genteel gentlemen and ladies would arrive by horse and buggy to purchase their prescriptions and assorted sundries at Apothecaries Hall Company, named in the manner of medieval English guilds by its founder, Dr. Gideon L. Platt.

But the store, which was founded in 1849, offered more than cosmetics and cold elixirs. Dr. Platt also distributed paint and industrial chemicals, a side of the business that prospered far beyond anyone's expectations, eventually becoming The Hubbard-Hall Chemical Company.

Today that name is synonymous with the accomplishment of providing the right solutions to fulfill the chemical needs of customers. But business at Hubbard-Hall is more than a matter of merely selling chemicals, according to Charles Kellogg, whose family has guided the firm's growth for seven generations. Rather, the firm is able to analyze a company's whole operation and make recommendations based on the customer's complete needs.

Hubbard-Hall is a manufacturer of specialty chemicals and a provider of related services in the eastern part of the country. Headquartered at 563 South Leonard Street, the firm also maintains facilities in Lincoln, Rhode Island, and Inman, South Carolina.

The corporation has evolved with the development of the city of Waterbury, changing to respond to the needs of the area. During the city's Brass Age, for example, the company supplied chemicals

such as sulfuric acid, chrome chemicals, and nickel anodes used in the production of brass.

The metal-finishing industry remains one of two major industries Hubbard-Hall supplies. The other is the electronics industry, a market that it has targeted since the onset of the printed circuit. The com-

Hubbard-Hall Inc. was founded in Waterbury, Connecticut, in 1849 as Apothecaries Hall Company. The name was changed to reflect the early changes in the product line, but ownership/management is now in the seventh generation of the same family.

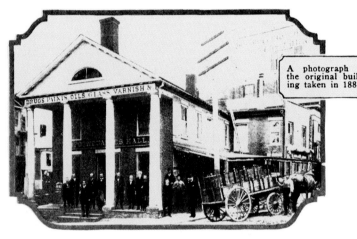

A photograph of the original building taken in 1885

pany is geared to meet the needs of high-tech manufacturers, providing the state-of-the-art reagents and laboratory-grade (purified) chemicals that are required in such modern manufacturing processes.

In addition to the manufacture of chemicals, Hubbard-Hall Inc. is the preeminent distributor of chemicals and services in the northeastern United States. The firm is able to offer its customers many advantages due to its dual role as a distributor and manufacturer. On the marketing end, for example, the company's field intelligence and coverage is immediate, allowing response time that can typically be measured in hours rather than days. It is able to cross-apply its expertise to handle customers' problems, as well as to suggest new applications. Hubbard-Hall is also able to offer more in the way of resources, including technical and support staff, laboratory and analytical capabilities, and regulatory

Hubbard-Hall Inc., located at 563 Leonard Street in Waterbury, not only manufactures chemicals but also is the preeminent distributor of chemicals and related services in the northeastern United States.

assistance.

The firm, which strives to be a good corporate citizen by complying with all regulations set forth by the government, also maintains a special H-HELP Division that sets up programs to train individuals within other companies who will in turn train their own employees in regulatory matters. Hubbard-Hall Inc. provides such services as up-to-the-minute information through computerized reports, as well as bulletins and newsletters on regulatory changes, compliance deadlines, and filling out forms.

The firm also brings to customers its expertise on environmental concerns, from helping to plan waste and toxicity reductions, to installing dikes with its own bulk tanks, to furnishing information about water-treatment technologies.

Other programs of Hubbard-Hall include both outside and in-house training in hazard communication, specific product safety, hazardous waste handling, and emergency response. The firm also offers specialized services such as in-plant total cleaning operation analysis and implementation of SPC (Statistic Process Control).

Some 30 percent of Hubbard-Hall Inc.'s stock is held by employees under a special Employee Stock Ownership Plan (ESOP) established in 1985 at no cost to the workers. This means that every employee is an owner, and is interested and involved in the firm's

This is a sampling of Hubbard-Hall's full-page, full-color ads that appear in a variety of national trade publications for the metal-finishing and printed circuit industries.

progress, assuring high-quality service.

This trend toward quality is certainly nothing new. Through the years Hubbard-Hall has seen the development of many successful ventures. In 1894 it erected a seven-story building that marked the advent of its entry into the drug wholesale business. In 1912 the company built an anode factory in Waterbury, and in 1920 erected a commercial fertilizer plant in East Windsor that produced a line of fertilizers under the Liberty brand for tobacco, potatoes, market gardens, and fruit orchards. As sales increased, so did those of the comparatively new in-

secticides and fungicides, and by the mid-1930s the firm was the largest jobber of these products in the nation.

With the rapid expansion of the farm business, the retail drug outlet was sold in 1950, and four years later the wholesale drug business as well. In 1957 three other fertilizer manufacturers joined the firm, which changed its name from Apothecaries Hall to The Hubbard-Hall Chemical Company and began to promote consumer fertilizers for lawns and gardens. In 1964 the firm was sold to the Kerr-McGee Corporation of Oklahoma City, one of America's largest corporations. The firm was purchased in 1966 by a group of Connecticut businessmen, including Hubbard-Hall executives, making it a wholly owned subsidiary of Rex Forge of Southington, Connecticut, which later changed its name to Connrex. In 1971 KKD Inc. purchased the assets of Hubbard-Hall from Connrex, changing its name to Hubbard-Hall Inc.

While the company's name changed several times, the chain of leadership was never broken since 1864, when it was purchased by Archibald E. Rice from founder Gideon L. Platt. Rice was current president Charles T. Kellogg's great-great-grandfather.

ANAMET INC.

It is not farfetched to suggest that Waterbury area residents come into contact with at least one Anamet component or product each day. The company's products are many and varied; in most cases they begin as stainless-steel strip that is formed into a stripwound hose, or welded into a long tube that is additionally corrugated to provide flexibility (the corrugations look and act very much like the bellows of an accordion). These are used to produce such items as flexible metal hose assemblies and expansion joints, which absorb movement in piping systems caused by thermal changes; vibration eliminators, which absorb vibration in air-conditioning and

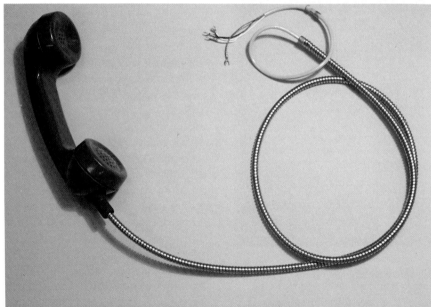

ABOVE: Anamet Inc. is engineering oriented and has been designing and producing metal hose and flexible tubing assemblies for more than 80 years. Shown here is a variety of the company's products.

LEFT: The flexible metal cord connecting the handset to the phonebox is an example of the many Anamet products.

refrigeration piping systems; and flexible stripwound, all-metal protective armor, designed to safeguard wiring and capillary tubing, along with a number of other products. In general, Anamet's products convey liquids or gasses at either temperature extreme and permit flexibility in piping systems.

While many have come into contact knowingly or otherwise with Anamet hoses and other products, likewise many have been acquainted with Anamet workers over the years. Traditionally one of the city's major employers, the firm began in 1908 as the American Metal Hose Company, a division of American Brass Company, located in New York City. Two years later the firm moved to Waterbury, where it transferred its corporate headquarters. In 1922 the Anaconda Company purchased the American Brass Company for $45 million, constituting, at the time, one of the largest purchases in U.S. industrial history.

The company continued to grow through the years, with major additions to both physical facilities and its product line. In the mid-1950s it constructed a plant in Illinois, doubling its size a decade later. European acquisitions began in the late 1960s.

Anaconda was acquired by the Atlantic Richfield Company in 1977. Three years later Anaconda Industries was formed as an Atlantic Richfield operating company, and Anaconda Metal Hose separated from the American Brass Company to become an Anaconda division in its own right. In 1984 Anamet Inc. was formed by several independent investors and many of the managers of Anaconda Metal Hose to become an independent company with its world headquarters in Waterbury. Today Anamet is a world leader within the metal hose industry, and its products find their way regularly to markets in more than 50 countries.

Anamet employs approximately 375 workers in Waterbury and has a second domestic plant in Mattoon, Illinois. Manufacturing operations also exist in Canada, Mexico, the United Kingdom, and the Netherlands. In recent times, in addition to considering more acquisitions, Anamet is focusing on seeking new product lines and expanding applications for existing ones. A broad-based corporation, at Anamet no single industrial segment accounts for more than 20 percent of its sales.

when you use a pay telephone, you could be using one of Anamet's products. The flexible metal cord connecting the handset to the phonebox is an example of the many Anamet products. Anamet is now a worldwide supplier of these connections for the communications industry.

The medical industry has also emerged as an opportunity for product applications. Anamet products are now found in operating rooms. A helically wound corrugated stainless assembly is produced and func-

ABOVE: The medical heat exchanger is a key part of the heart/lung life-support equipment used in cardiopulmonary surgery.

LEFT: Sealtite®, flexible, liquidtite, electrical wiring conduit, is manufactured to comply with a variety of international standards.

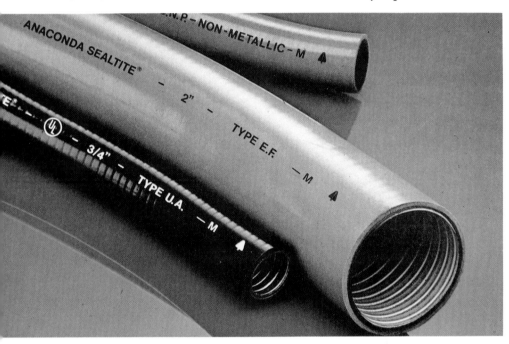

The company is engineering oriented, designing and producing metal hose and flexible tubing assemblies for more than 80 years. Its long-term experience in working with various metals and materials provides a solid background for Anamet's present hose capabilities. The company has also accumulated a wealth of information regarding field installations involving flexible connectors for pipe movement.

For more than eight decades the firm has led the way in the area of flexible products, making its mark not only on the Waterbury landscape, but in marketplaces worldwide.

Did you ever consider that

tions as a component of a lung oxygenator unit, and serves as a key part in the heart/lung life-support equipment used in cardiopulmonary surgery. The heat exchanger is used to lower and control the blood temperature during open-heart surgery.

The automotive industry is also an end user of Anamet products. The firm's products absorb the expansion forces and repeated heat/cool cycle stresses in the stainless-steel tubular manifold systems. Corrugated hoses are supplied for oil-drain lines, exhaust connectors, manifold bellows, exhaust gas-recirculating hoses, and, in addition, a great variety of strip-

wound hoses are used for numerous applications.

The company began addressing the electrical industry in the 1940s by providing products for flexible connections to motor leads and for connections within panel boxes. The firm offers Sealtite® conduit. Sealtite is the original flexible, liquidtite, electrical wiring conduit, and now is manufactured to comply with a variety of international standards and is produced in all of Anamet's international locations. A thermoplastic cover is extruded over a flexible galvanized steel core to protect the wires from corrosive fumes, abrasion, oil, grease, water, dirt, and chemicals. The company now also produces nonmetallic conduit for this industry. In keeping with Anamet's policy of identifying emerging applications, the computer industry offers potential by using conduit to connect computer wiring networks within the subflooring of computer rooms.

MACDERMID INCORPORATED

MacDermid Incorporated was founded in Waterbury by a Scottish immigrant in 1922. His very first product was Metex Metal Cleaner No. 1, which found a thriving market in the booming rolled brass industry of the Naugatuck Valley. It saved countless hours of tedious hand scrubbing and polishing, and gained wide acceptance as an economical means of preparing metal parts for subsequent plating operations.

Since that time the company has expanded to more than 800 employees worldwide, more than 1,000 products, and sales that exceed $140 million. After a five-year, $8-million renovation of the research and technical complex on Freight Street, gleaming, state-of-the-art laboratories give the company a space-age look. Sophisticated process-control instrumentation and computerized testing equipment help chemists in their trade. Customers from major firms worldwide meet regularly in MacDermid's stylish boardrooms for technical training and product updates.

Through the years MacDermid has been a true innovator in its field. For example, the company developed the first reverse current alkaline cleaner for steel in 1938. The product, Anodex, propelled MacDermid into the automotive industry and opened up new national markets.

Expansion became the established pattern of MacDermid over the years. The firm's early expertise in metal finishing enabled it to adapt readily to the new surface technology requirements of the P.C. board of the early 1960s. Another natural extension of MacDermid's expertise in surface finishing was plating on plastics for automotive, appliance, and plumbing applications. In the late 1970s an aggressive research and product development program allowed MacDermid to enter the semiconductor market with a line of ultrapure

photoresists used in the manufacture of integrated circuits. Today MacDermid boasts the most diverse line of specialty chemicals for the metal-finishing, printed circuit, and semiconductor industries.

The company continued to grow both financially and geographically. In the early 1970s direct operations were formed to service the European market. The Asian market then began to show signs of growth, and independent business centers were opened to serve the needs of that marketplace. Mac-Dermid's specialty chemicals have gained wide acceptance throughout these major world markets.

Today the firm maintains facilities in Canada, Great Britain, West

MacDermid Incorporated is at the forefront of chemical-processing technology for electronics and microelectronics applications.

Germany, Spain, France, Switzerland, Italy, Israel, the Netherlands, Finland, Sweden, South Africa, Japan, Korea, Taiwan R.O.C., Hong Kong, Singapore, Australia, Brazil, Argentina, Venezuela, Mexico, and Puerto Rico.

MacDermid's goal is to create an industry image that automatically prompts people in the industries they serve to think first of MacDermid and to justify that thought by thinking first of the customers' needs. MacDermid's philosophy of Complete Cycle

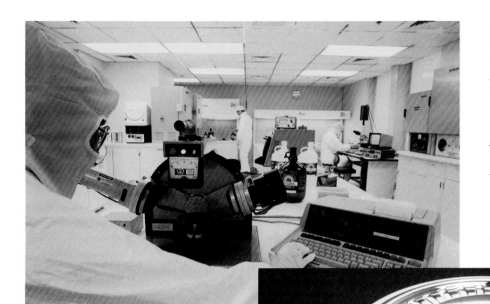

LEFT: MacDermid's microelectronic chemicals, manufactured and tested under the most stringent conditions, are used in the production of multimegabit semiconductors.

BELOW LEFT: MacDermid's 10,000-square-foot customer service lab for metal finishing and electronic product testing and process simulation.

BELOW: MacDermid's metal-finishing processes are used in a variety of industries, including automotive, plumbing, appliance, and furniture.

Responsibility® necessitates that products, technical service, and control instrumentation all be available to suit customers' individual requirements. The MacDermid philosophy asks the employees: "What are the customers' needs?" and "how do we best serve those needs?"

Obviously, the answers lie in selling quality products that help the customer today and tomorrow, and in consistently offering high-quality technical support. Instead of innovation for the sake of innovation, MacDermid directs its research and technical service efforts toward the needs of the customer. "What's right for the customer is right for MacDermid" is the underlying motto by which the people of MacDermid live.

The slogan could be carried one step further. "What's right for the employees is right for the company." In other words, the people are MacDermid. The firm was sold to the employees in 1959, and today more than 85 percent of them own shares in the company, giving them a special interest in the progress and profit of both the business and the customer.

The crux—and the heart—of the firm is its people, from top management down to the newest employees. MacDermid places its faith in entrepreneurs and innovators. It strives to attract people with creative and probing minds, encouraging employees to have the "guts to fail."

The advantage of this and the importance of the employees are perhaps best summed up by quoting from MacDermid Incorporated's corporate philosophy: "Our progress, our company's long-term advantage, and your long-term advantage lie in our human resources. Other advantages that come about from technological improvements, the opening of new markets, lower costs, all prove to be relatively short-run. So, it is the initiative, the will, and the motivation people bring to their work that we have to rely upon for survival and growth."

AIRPAX COMPANY,
A DIVISION OF NORTH AMERICAN PHILIPS CORP.

The planet Earth, with its land masses and oceans, is an overwhelming "backyard" for many companies, but Airpax Company, a Cheshire-based firm, bridges cultures and countries, manufacturing and marketing on a global basis.

A progressive, people-oriented firm, Airpax maintains three manufacturing facilities in Cheshire, as well as two in Maryland and one each in Brussels, Mexico, and Singapore. The company has two joint ventures in Japan, of which it retains 50-percent ownership, and also has distribution and marketing centers in West Germany, Sweden, and England.

The firm attributes its above-average growth rate to its highly engineered, state-of-the-art products, many of which are slated for the information systems markets, including computers, office automation, and telecommunications. The automotive arena is also a significant marketplace for Airpax. Much of the growth in automotive can be attributed to the electronics being added to today's automobiles.

Airpax designs and manufactures electronic and electromechanical products that protect, monitor, and control. By being sensitive to

Airpax engineers utilize computer-aided design (CAD) to create precision products.

customer and employee needs and dedicated to technological development, the firm strives to provide the highest-quality products and services at a competitive price.

Airpax believes that growth occurs as a result of fulfilling the need for customer requirements. In the early days of the firm, which was founded in 1945 as The A.W. Haydon Company, some 95 percent of its focus was on the military aerospace industry.

By the early 1950s it was becoming evident that market diversification was necessary if the firm was to continue to grow.

The new emphasis was now on commercial applications, with increased efforts on research and development to create products to fit these needs. A concentrated program for the next 15 years brought a dramatic change in products and targeted markets. Penetration was made into, for example, the computer peripheral, telecommunications, medical instrumentation, and other markets.

During the early 1970s the company changed its name to North American Philips Controls Corp. A new facility was constructed in the Cheshire Industrial Park in 1972. Various acquisitions were made in the 1970s, and the firm's product line was greatly expanded. New products being produced included magnetic circuit breakers, microcircuit packages, speed sensors, tachometers, and thermostats. By 1978 "Airpax" was adapted as a trade name for all products.

Behind all the expansions, the additions of facilities, and the acquisitions has been Airpax' commitment to satisfy customer needs. Since the firm's inception it has worked directly with the design engineers of major manufacturers to develop new product concepts or to modify existing products to fit alternative applications.

As an example, Airpax manufactured a digital linear actuator in re-

sponse to the automotive manufacturers' need to more efficiently control the fuel and air mixture in a fuel-injection system. The digital linear actuator will, upon command, open or close a small air passage to accomplish the proper balance. This process is controlled by a computer chip that sends a signal to activate the process. Airpax digital linear actuators convert the rotary motion of stepper motors into precise, bidirectional linear movements. Other appli-

A digital linear actuator that controls the air/fuel mixture in an automotive throttle body system.

cations can be found, for example, in the medical instrumentation field, where they are used in intravenous feeders, blood analyzers, and CAT scanner lens control.

Airpax design capabilities are backed by modern manufacturing methods. The firm has made heavy capital investments in tooling and automation equipment. Robotics, for example, is used extensively in the manufacturing process, as are high-speed production systems.

Airpax considers people its greatest resource, with skill and ability being the most important hiring criteria. The company's philosophy is that pride of workmanship and, in turn, superior product quality, comes from providing employees with the latest equipment and the kind of environment in which they can learn and grow.

Education is a critical element in Airpax' employee policies. Frequent training sessions are held to upgrade employee skills, and the company offers a college reimbursement program for job-related courses.

Airpax strives to recognize outstanding employee performance and has a special Employee of the Month Award. One of the perks of being so named is use of a specially designated parking spot in the parking lot.

Airpax believes in advancements from within, and when a new position opens, the job is first posted internally. The management tries to maintain an open-door policy, to treat all employees equally, and to encourage employees to find increasingly challenging positions within the company. In other words, Airpax tries to furnish the opportunity for its workers to build their careers within the firm.

Special awards are given for years of service, with many employees having reached more than 25 years of service. Employees are

The Airpax manufacturing facility in the Cheshire Industrial Park, Cheshire.

encouraged to become active within their community, to serve various causes and take part in the Red Cross Blood Mobile and the YMCA fund raiser among others.

By fostering such a healthy atmosphere for its employees, Airpax believes it has created a team approach that translates into a higher quality product and a better company overall.

Needless to say, Airpax has not gone unnoticed in the world marketplace. Its influence can be felt in virtually every corner of the world, with the production of an amazing array of products. For example, it manufactures sensors used in the fuel tanks of recreational vehicles, stepper motors to position paper feed in printers, and linear actuators to position read/write heads in floppy and hard disk drives.

Another interesting example of the applications of Airpax motors is in Automatic Teller Machines. The firm manufactures the motor that takes and then gives back the customer's plastic card.

One new area being explored by Airpax is the manufacture of electronic-controlled dampers for forced-air heating and air conditioning. This is a sophisticated electronics system operated by a central motor.

The company is also the world leader in the manufacture of magnetic circuit breakers. These

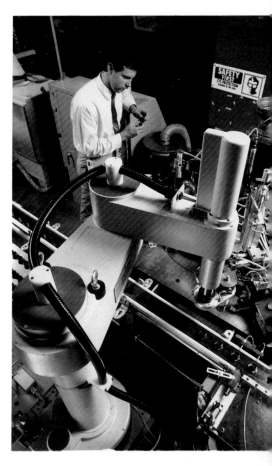

Use of robotics results in faster, accurate, and more efficient production.

are primarily used in electronics applications, including computers. Essentially, circuit breakers protect expensive instruments from potentially being damaged due to high-voltage conditions.

Other Airpax products include speed sensors, which are used in jet engines to monitor the speed of the turbine, and thermostats, which prevent overheating conditions in applications ranging from a huge road grader to intricate electronic circuitry in a computer.

A variety of control components are manufactured in Cheshire, including digital linear actuators, brushless DC motors, indicators and sensors, and tachometers. Such products find applications in virtually every corner of the globe, controlling and/or monitoring applications in everything from CAT scans to computers.

LEWIS ELECTRONIC INSTRUMENTATION DIVISION/COLT

In 1927 the miracle of flight was harnessed for the paying public; the first scheduled commercial air flight was successfully completed, a part of the United States Postal Service.

Meanwhile, in Connecticut, another enterprise was getting off the ground, the Naugatuck Engineering Machine Company, which was to become the Lewis Engineering Company and finally Lewis Electronic Instrumentation, a firm whose growth has been directly linked to the aviation industry.

Three years after the firm was founded in 1925, it began devoting its attention primarily to the aircraft market. From wartime to peacetime markets, the company grew, becoming an acknowledged leader in the manufacture of a wide range of instruments. In 1944 it embarked on a new venture—the production of special wire and cable that would resist exposure to a wide variety of environmental conditions. A wire mill was built in 1960 on Spring Street, and the business greatly expanded, until it was sold in the early 1970s.

The main emphasis throughout the years, however, has been on instrumentation—the manufacture of products on the cutting

edge. Today Lewis instruments are displaying more than mere temperatures. They are monitoring pressure, flow, revelations per minute, vibration, position, voltage, liquid level, torque, acceleration, and other conditions.

One of the top five companies of its kind in the world, Lewis enjoys a global marketplace. Its instruments can be found on virtually every major commercial airline, as well as on many of the smaller ones. Roughly 75 percent of the firm's business is geared to the commercial market, with the remainder devoted to the military marketplace.

From design to production, from inductive soldering to critical operations such as the attachment of hair springs to the armature assembly, all key functions are conducted under Lewis' uncompromising quality control, offering precision and reliability that is unrivaled.

Lewis was acquired by Colt Industries in 1985 and became part of its Aerospace/Government Segment. Its Naugatuck plant has more than 45,000 square feet of administration, engineering, quality-assurance, laboratory, and

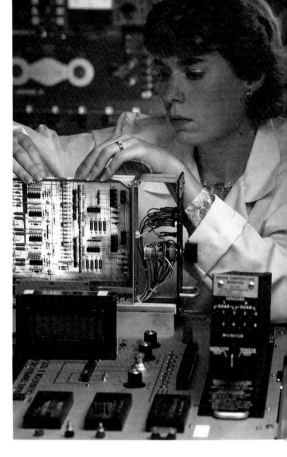

A technician works on a PC board for the brake temperature monitor primarily used on the Boeing 757 and 767.

manufacturing functions, offering such in-house capabilities as tooling, machine shop, plating, and dial fabricating.

Lewis Electronic Instrumentation today enjoys a worldwide reputation for working with aerospace systems engineering to implement requirements in the areas of digital interfacing, signal conditioning, microprocessor-based systems, cockpit instruments, custom packaging, and environmental testing. And the Lewis name on the product means that it has been qualified to exacting standards, keeping pace with today's demanding aviation industry.

LEFT: A fuel quantity gauge, which is typically used on smaller commuter airliners.

BELOW: Typical temperature transducers used on every commercial airliner.

AMERICAN CHEMICAL & REFINING CO., INC.

There's gold in the hills of Waterbury—at American Chemical & Refining Co., Inc., to be exact. ACR is a major manufacturer of gold and silver proprietary plating materials and processes.

Incorporated in 1948 as a refiner of gold and a producer of gold salts for use in electroplating, the company's processes have applications today in many areas, with the electronic marketplace accounting for about 85 percent of its activity. ACR is involved in several other industries, including solar energy systems, defense products, space exploration, and the decorative market and jewelry.

to the company that can provide the best technical service—an accomplishment that ACR prides itself on. ACR also stands for accurate, consistent, and reliable.

In addition to the products that account for about half of the Waterbury firm's business, ACR has a sophisticated recovery process designed to recover gold and palladium, which are obtained from such sources as spent plating solutions, sludges, and filters.

The plating process, for example, is not 100-percent efficient. A large amount of the metal being plated is not absorbed directly onto the part. Because of the value

Through the years the company, which is the largest producer of silver salt in the nation, has added a number of products to its basic line, including base metal processes for acid copper, bright acid tin, and electroless copper for PTH applications.

What distinguishes ACR from other companies of its type is its technical expertise. In a highly competitive marketplace, business goes

of precious metals, it is cost effective to recover such remaining substances in the plating effluent or "spent" solution. ACR has developed a special method, using some of its proprietary processes as well as conventional practices, to recover such material.

Another aspect of ACR, which is headquartered at 36 Sheffield Street and maintains other facilities and offices in the United

States and Europe, is the company's ability to perform analytical services on a contractual basis. It provides, for example, complex chemical analysis of plating solutions, effluent, and product discharges. It can provide critical information for any company that has to meet water discharge limits. Due to ever-growing environmental restrictions, contracted analytical analysis is an expanding part of the firm's business.

The addition of this service is also indicative of the firm's continued growth in order to meet the needs of a changing market, an ability it has maintained since 1948. American Chemical & Refining Co., Inc., has become a leader in the production of specialty precious metal chemicals and metal-finishing equipment and in providing complete technical service to the metal-finishing industry.

THE SIEMON COMPANY

When The Siemon Company was founded in 1903, computers were still in the realm of science fiction and it had been fewer than 30 years since Alexander Graham Bell invented the telephone and spoke those immortal words, "Mr. Watson, come here. I want you."

And while throughout its long history Siemon has made everything from umbrellas to mousetraps, it is those two areas—computers and telecommunications—to which the firm today devotes its attention.

Siemon's main product, which is referred to in the industry as a "66 connection system" or a "quick clip," is designed to assist in the distribution of a wide variety of information. It carries signals as opposed to power.

A rough analogy would be to compare it to a plumbing system. In such a system water enters the building and the plumbing that feeds the building is broken out at different points to distribute the water to various end users. In the Siemon system, the telephone or data-communication lines enter the building and are terminated on a Siemon connector, then cross connected to various switching equipment and workstations where individual telephones and computers are installed.

Siemon provides the broadest line of 66 connectors in the world, along with supporting auxiliary hardware. The company has devoted the past quarter-century to producing such systems for the telecommunications industry, for which it has established the wire-management standard. The computer marketplace has opened up in recent times, and now use of the firm's product for computer applications is almost as widespread as in the telephone industry.

Throughout the company's history innovation has been the rule of thumb. The firm was founded by Carl F. Siemon, a native of Fort Wayne, Indiana, who experimented

with plastics. After many trials he developed a composition that could withstand heat and boiling water and that was extremely durable, lending itself to the manufacture of handles for carving knives. He moved to the East in 1898 to take a managerial position in a rubber company, and eventually formed a partnership with Waldo C. Bryant, founder of Bryant Electric Company, to open the Siemon Hard Rubber Company in February 1903. That organization eventually became The Siemon Company.

At the time, the firm was the fifth-oldest plastic molder in the United States, and produced, among other items, phonographic records for Decca and Victor Record Company. In 1906 The Siemon Company became involved with AT&T, formerly Western Electric, and has become the oldest continuous supplier to that firm.

Throughout the years Siemon has developed many "breakthrough" products, such as a molding compound nicknamed by the company "Connecticut River Mud." Its strength, high resistance to heat, and low water absorption made it well suited for electrical and telecommunications applications.

Siemon, however, is not only on the leading edge in terms of its product but also in terms of production. It has recently implemented a complex MRPII (Manufacturing Resource Planning system) that ties together via computer all the various aspects of a business, including ac-

Carl Siemon, chairman of the board.

counting, engineering, purchasing, production, scheduling, and capacity forecasting. The system in essence automates the information flow, providing to-the-minute feedback about all aspects of its manufacturing resources.

Furthermore, the system links together Siemon's four major divisions. All divisions are located in Watertown—Siemon Molding, which manufactures precision molded parts for Siemon products and for outside customers; Siemon Dynamic, which produces tooling and precision metal stampings and formings; Siemon Electronics, which specializes in wire and cable harness assembly; and Siemon Assembly, which assembles, packages, and stocks Siemon Company products.

The firm is headquartered in Watertown at the Siemon Business Park, in a complex that was origi-

ABOVE: Carl N. Siemon (seated), president, and brothers (from left), Henry, John, and C.K., carry on the company tradition of service and innovation. Photo by Robert Hauser

LEFT: Vertical integration of services allows direct product development through all stages, from design through manufacture.

RIGHT: Some of the many "wiring solution" products manufactured by The Siemon Company.

nally the Princeton Knitting Mill. Long a town eyesore, Siemon purchased the facility in 1984 and began extensive renovations. The firm transformed the mill complex into the region's first "intelligent" building. Siemon Business Park tenants have shared access to services that include an advanced phone system, CAD/CAM system, data processing, FAX, and Voice Mail. The building now houses, in addition to the firm's own headquarters and two of its divisions, some eight other corporations.

And while The Siemon Company boasts many high-technology advantages, it believes that its best resources are its people and relies, to a large extent, on homegrown talent. The firm tries, whenever possible, to promote from within, posting job openings in the plant prior to using outside advertising.

Siemon's philosophy is to foster employee awareness of the whole operation, and promote employees' consideration of their ability to move in various directions.

Thus the work force, in essence, is multifunctional, with employees able to do several different jobs. This approach leads to a higher level of quality consciousness, Siemon believes.

The family-owned company is under the guidance of Carl N. Siemon, a graduate of Yale University. In 1982 he became the fourth Carl Siemon in a row to hold the office of company president. According to Carl N. Siemon, customer service is the highest priority at Siemon. He and his brothers—Henry, John, and C.K.—work together to expand on the company's tradition of service and innovation. Their father, Carl, is active as the chairman of the board of directors.

The firm also maintains strong ties with the Watertown community. It provides, for example, a scholarship program started in

1949 for Watertown High School students that yearly sponsors six different scholarships. The Siemon Company also provides a scholarship fund for Spaulding High School in Rochester, New Hampshire, and one for The Choate School in Wallingford, Connecticut. The company believes that education is what keeps both the community and the country strong and that it is also the means of upward mobility.

From its community involvement to its employee commitment to its emphasis on service for its space-age products, The Siemon Company is clearly a leading force in the communications industry, with roots that reach back to 1903.

THE PLATT BROTHERS & CO.

A mighty bridge, its girders glistening in the sun, spans both banks of a river, providing a passageway for thousands of cars every day. But an unseen enemy attacks—corrosion.

Billions of dollars virtually corrode away on U.S. highway bridges and other steel structures each year. Much of this staggering waste could be avoided with proper corrosion protection. Zinc metallizing, a versatile process in which zinc wire is fed into a gun with oxygen and an acetylene flame, melted, and then sprayed, is one solution offered by The Platt Brothers & Co.

At Platt, they think zinc. The Waterbury firm is involved in supplying a variety of specialized zinc materials, prominent among them its own "Plattline™," a steel-cored, zinc rod that is used for, among other things, corrosion prevention along the entire underground portion of the 800-mile Alaskan pipeline. This material is welded in lengths along both sides of the pipe and sacrifices itself, dissolving to protect the steel around it from rusting in the current-conducting earth.

Zinc metallizing is used for steel fencing, deck structures, concrete pipe joint rings, and gas bottles—any place where rusting can occur through exposure to the elements or to corrosive materials.

Another special Platt zinc product is used in the global automotive market in making a streamlined fuse, called a blade style fuse. Zinc strip, likewise, is a major component of electrical

LEFT: Platt Brothers produces a variety of wrought-zinc products.

BELOW: The Eyelet Division manufactures several types of drawn metal parts.

Plattline™ Ribbon Anodes provide a simple, maintenance-free method of cathodic protection.

fuses, as it is a reasonably good resistor of electricity and has a relatively low melting temperature, so it will disintegrate before other materials.

Platt makes zinc in strip, rod, wire, and shaped forms. The company's single-largest product is zinc metallizing wire, used in the metallizing process for protecting such structural steel forms as bridges, lock gates, flood-control gates, underwater structures, towers, mine structures, buildings, and wrought-iron furniture.

A process that Platt calls ahead of its time, zinc metallizing rapidly propels the molten zinc particles onto a prepared substrate, creating a layered coating.

When a structure is protected by painting, by contrast, pockets of rust form when a scratch occurs on the painted steel. These corrosion pits and blisters will continue

to grow. In the zinc metallizing process, a zinc-metallized coating "sacrifices" itself by galvanic action when scratched, and such action will continue as long as any zinc remains in the area.

Another interesting use for Platt zinc is for the divider strips used in terrazzo flooring. This special strip features a top section of zinc and a bottom section of galvanized steel. The company offers them in more than 15 variations and designs, including some that are completely zinc.

The Platt Brothers & Co. favors value-added products, creating many new products at the request of customers, often even designing and building new machinery to manufacture the new product.

In addition to the zinc phase of operations, the firm also has a drawn metal parts division, where it produces eyelet and press parts and maintains a fully staffed Design Engineering and Tooling Department, geared to meet customer needs. Through the utilization of its many years of expertise, the Platt professionals can often eliminate many costly secondary operations by designing them into production tooling.

While Platt carries a limited line of standard eyelets, the major thrust of this end of the business comes from producing drawn metal parts to customer specifications. Products include parts for fluorescent light tubes, automotive products, sensing devices, counting and metering equipment, and even arrow tips.

The company has, through the years, proven itself as both a pioneer and an innovator. It is the granddaddy of Waterbury companies, tracing its origins back almost two centuries, when it got its start with a sawmill on the Naugatuck River. Metal buttons were another of its chief products for a significant part of its history.

The Platt family came to Waterbury in 1797, when Nathan Platt bought land on the banks of the Naugatuck, in the area still referred to as Platt's Mill or Plattsville. He built a home for his family there and improvised a dam across the river, which supplied power for a sawmill. The mill could also be converted to grind grist for the Platt family and friends.

When the river waters undermined the makeshift dam, Platt rebuilt it, also adding three new mills, one of them a combination foundry and machine shop in which he and his son, Leonard, built a wire-making and button-eye business. Older brother Alfred was the founder of various firms that evolved into The Platt Brothers & Co. His son, William S. Platt, is credited with setting the business on its current course, supervising the production of a significant amount of rolled zinc.

Business boomed during the Civil War, when the firm made uniform buttons and the small zinc disks used in bullets. It continued to grow, and in the twentieth century Platt abandoned the button industry to concentrate on zinc. During the great flood of 1955, the company's riverside buildings were destroyed, and the firm built its new plant at South Main Street, to which it has made many additions since.

And through it all, from the time the first Platt set foot in Waterbury to today, when the firm is a recognized world leader in its field, The Platt Brothers & Co. has provided customers in all corners of the globe with quality materials and components, with timely service, and with the latest in manufacturing methods.

Platt Brothers today and in 1878 (inset).

SUMMIT CORPORATION OF AMERICA

Summit Corporation of America is an undeniable leader in the electroplating industry. In the state-of-the-art laboratory of its high-technology testing facilities, Summit's research and development specialists are creating materials systems and products that meet and exceed performance requirements of today—and tomorrow.

Systems such as SCA's Fired Catalytic™ Electrometallization, a ceramic-board metallizing system featuring high-density copper conductors and terminations derived via electrometallurgical techniques, are today's answer to the constantly changing needs of the electroplating industry.

Ceramics are considered by many to be the material of the future, and Summit is ready today

One of the largest electroplating companies in the world, Summit Corporation of America is headquartered in Thomaston.

S.E.M. stage.

with systems that they will be able to expand and modify to meet evolving needs.

Whether a product involves leading-edge technology or traditional plating processes, SCA's commitment is a solid one, based on a philosophy that its owners, managers, and employees live in the communities in which the firm operates and are in business "for the long run."

At the heart of SCA's environmental concerns is an engineered environmental program designed to conserve, reclaim, and recycle resources, as well as to meet or exceed federal and state regulations. A staff of environmental engineers works at each of the plants, sharing ideas, data, and information, and each SCA operation has extensive education and training programs for employees.

The firm's Toxicology Program is truly a step into the future of environmental management. The program provides a critical research and development tool that allows SCA not only to effectively treat current waste, but to conduct research on more effective methods of treatment, conservation, reclamation, and recycling. The ultimate goal of the SCA Toxicology Program is theoretical zero discharge.

SCA is committed to preserving the quality product, maintaining a comprehensive quality-assurance program, as well as conducting a complete testing of final product on the premises—testing that includes, but is not limited to, straightness, strip width, thickness, and strip pitch.

SCA maintains an active research and development department, often working with customers in partnership programs, setting up a dedicated team to work in conjunction with a client's research group thus creating processes to meet future requirements.

Innovation is an underlying philosophy of SCA, a firm committed to providing customers with the latest and most cost-effective technology available. Such a system, for example, is a palladium/nickel and gold flash-plating system, which allows reduced-gold plating, resulting in reduced cost without compromising product quality. Compared to the typical gold-only plating, this method offers lower and more stable cost, lower porosity, better wear resistance, and better resistance to a variety of corrosion modes such as humidity, salt, sulfide, and chloride. It also maintains equivalent performance in contact and frictional resistance and fretting oxidation.

Summit Corporation provides a wide variety of plating systems. It is, for example, a major supplier of electroplated lead frames to the microelectronics market. These include transistors, integrated circuits, power rectifiers, hall effect devices, electro-optic couplers, and microwave systems.

A pioneer in the area of reel-to-reel plating and working in that segment of the industry, SCA's experience with precision plated ma-

SCA is committed to responsible environmental management both as a corporate goal and a reality.

terials has grown to include such applications as thermal fuses for automobiles, batteries, antennae for radar and space communications, and conductor ground planes for telephone and electrical hookups.

SCA also features barrel plating, utilizing the latest type of vibratory baskets for both stationary and in-line plating. Each day literally millions of small pins and contact and thermal devices are plated with tin, silver, nickel, gold, and palladium by the company. The firm also offers rack plating, depositing silver or copper up to .035 of an inch thick.

SCA's headquarters in Thomaston includes a prototype and development laboratory along with a complete production facility. It also has plants in Indianapolis, Indiana, and in Mountain View and Hayward, California—some 240,000 square feet in all. SCA has sales agents in the United States, Europe, and Asia, including Hong Kong, Korea, Singapore, Taiwan, and Thailand.

One of the largest electroplating companies in the world, Summit Corporation of America is setting the standard for the industry, backed by its many years of expertise.

Vibratory plating.

RISDON CORPORATION

The world of cosmetics is one of glitz and ritz, where fragrances, lipsticks, toiletries, and other essentials are often showcased in gleaming, sleek containers of Risdon Corporation's design and production.

The package is an intregal part of the product, and, in this respect, Risdon Corporation of Naugatuck plays a major role in the multibillion-dollar cosmetics and toiletries industry. Risdon designs and produces high-fashion cosmetics and toiletries packaging for Avon, Revlon, Estée Lauder, Bristol-Myers, and other such companies whose products can be found on department store shelves and in the homes and purses of millions of women worldwide.

Whether they are shaped like gems or fluted with gold, these caps, cases, and other component parts add glamour, elegance, and functionality to a variety of lipsticks, fragrances, mascaras, and other products.

The world's largest producer of such packaging and components, Risdon has capabilities in plastics molding, metal fabricating and finishing, decorating and assembly, dispensing systems manufacturing, vacuum metalizing, and brush making. A multimillion-dollar corporation, Risdon also makes customized fabricated metal components for other consumer and industrial markets.

More than one-half of the firm's 1,800 employees work in three Connecticut locations—at Risdon's headquarters and Metal Cosmetics Division in Naugatuck, at the Cosmetic Container Division in Danbury, and at the Fragrance and Dispensing Systems Division in Thomaston. Risdon also has five additional facilities in the United States and Canada, as well as affiliates in Europe and in Mexico.

The firm was founded in 1910, when a group of 114 Connecticut citizens gathered at the Naugatuck Town Hall, concerned that

their small community would never prosper if it were to depend soley on the seasonal employment its rubber footwear mills offered. These residents raised $25,000 to purchase a small Waterbury toolworks company owned by Sidney A. Risdon, and over the years the firm manufactured a wide range of products, among them kerosene lamp burners, electrical appliances, and even pistol cartridge clips made during the two world wars. The company's current emphasis on cosmetics packaging started to take shape in the 1940s, when Risdon began assembling lipstick containers in volume and essentially transformed its traditional styling into a glamour item.

Risdon Corporation designs and produces a wide variety of packaging and components for cosmetics and toiletries.

The firm grew to provide a full line of cosmetics packaging. In 1978 MB Group plc of Reading, England, acquired Risdon as a means of marketing cosmetics and toiletries packaging on a global basis. In 1989 Risdon became part of CMB Packaging of Brussels, Belgium, the world's third-largest packaging company.

From its roots deep in the Naugatuck Valley, Risdon Corporation today offers innovative, high-quality packaging, spray pumps, and other parts—providing a touch of glamour to the world.

THE EASTERN COMPANY

The Eastern Company, which today makes everything from locks to fasteners to support the roofs of underground mines, is a $75-million-plus public corporation that owes its healthy start in the nineteenth century to Yankee ingenuity.

Back in 1834 Eben Tuttle, a young Naugatuck foundryman, took a fresh look at an old farming instrument—the hoe. This agricultural basic had not been changed in virtually thousands of years. Its square iron blade affixed at right angles to a wooden handle rendered it unwieldly for its intended purpose of close chopping around the roots of plants. Furthermore, Tuttle knew, its rigidity made for back-breaking work.

His creativity lead to the invention and patenting of the gooseneck hoe, with a springy gooseneck interpositioned between neck and handle, now a staple of gardeners and farmers.

Eben Tuttle's small foundry was a direct predecessor of The Eastern Company, founded in 1858 by his son, Bronson Beecher Tuttle, and his partner, John Howard Whittemore. The Tuttles and Whittemores are families well known throughout the history of Naugatuck. Donald S. Tuttle III is the seventh generation of Tuttles to serve on the company's board of directors, a feat unique in corporate America. The Whittemores are currently represented by R.N. Whittemore, also a member of the board of directors.

Those early ancestors of the organization would look with awe at the company Eastern has become. Begun as a producer of iron farm implements, as well as castings for the horse-and-carriage trade, the firm's product mix changed with the nation's economy, adjusting to the times and to the industrialization of America with a broad array of metal parts. It made, for example, armaments during the Civil War, hardware for harness- and wagon-makers, parts for the railroads during their golden age, and later, with the advent of the horseless carriage, parts for automobiles. The company produced literally hundreds of parts for the Maxwell—the car so beloved by Jack Benny.

After World War II the operation shifted its emphasis toward more updated markets. Today the company has several major product lines: high-security and electric switch locks for industrial and electronic equipment, proprietary latching devices, security fasteners for mine roof supports, concrete construction materials, and iron and high-alloy steel castings.

The firm has also greatly expanded throughout the years, acquiring and adding divisions in eight different locations in the United States and in Canada and Taiwan.

The Eastern Company's philosophy is to be a domineering factor in niche markets instead of being one of many players in big markets. The firm has traditionally maintained a strong financial position that is underscored by the fact that it has paid consecutive quarterly dividends since 1940, only one of a few publicly traded coporations to do so.

This illustration by B.B. Tuttle, co-founder of The Eastern Company with J.H. Whittemore in 1858, depicts the original iron foundry on the Naugatuck River, now the site of Alloy Foundries and Eastern's headquarters.

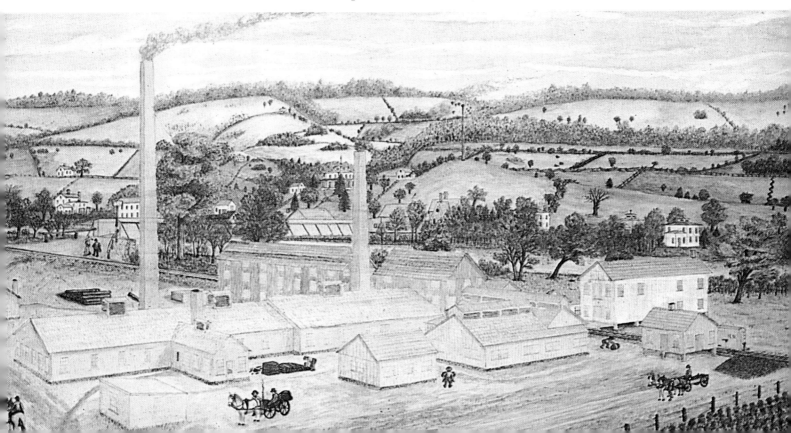

TRUELOVE & MACLEAN INC.

Thomas Truelove and Donald Maclean formed a partnership in 1944 to enter into the metal goods business. For the first several years the two toolmakers worked 75 or more hours weekly, building tools and dies while production equipment was being obtained for manufacturing.

Operations started in a rented loft, but with the prosperity that followed the war, the company was able to erect its own building in 1946, and many additions have been constructed since that time. The firm now has a modern facility where a wide range of stampings and deep-drawn parts are produced.

The flood of 1955 left Truelove & Maclean unharmed, but severe damage occurred during the tornado in 1962. Some sections of the plant had to be completely torn down and rebuilt, but, with unlimited assistance from many local firms, everything was back to normal promptly.

The company attributes much of its success to the availability of capable personnel. A majority of its journeymen have been trained in the plant, and many have spent their entire working careers there. Top management and supervisory employees are all skilled tradesmen.

T&M has a wide range of customers throughout the United States and in many foreign countries. Some have been with the company for almost its entire existence. Among the industries served are automotive, battery, cosmetic, electrical, electronic, furniture, hardware, lighting, medical, and ordnance.

Bouffard Metal Goods Inc. in Watertown, which is engaged in the same type of manufacturing, is an affiliate of Truelove & Maclean Inc. The two companies continue their policy of expansion and refinement in order to meet the ever-changing needs of their customers.

BRISTOL BABCOCK INC.

Thomas Edison visited there. So did Henry Ford.

Even early in its history, Bristol Babcock Inc., founded in 1889 as the Bristol's Manufacturing Company and later known as the Bristol Company, was well recognized in the field of instrumentation. Today the founder of electricity and the automobile magnate would hardly recognize the company Bristol Babcock has become—a leader and an innovator in the field of high-technology instrumentation and control systems that were once unimaginable.

The firm originally manufactured steel belt lacing and recording pressure gauges. By the early 1890s the company had already introduced several recording instruments to the industrial marketplace, including the first practical thermocouples and the pyrometer, a fundamental instrument in today's technology. Such pioneering efforts have never ceased. In 1975 Bristol Babcock introduced the UCS 3000, the first microprocessor-based control system.

Communications products are a major focus of the company, formerly a division of Acco Industries Inc. and now a subsidiary of Babcock Industries Inc. Recognizing the importance of communications in both telecontrol and distributed control networks, Bristol Babcock Inc. offers a variety of choices for virtually any application.

Bristol Babcock's main office and production facility in Watertown.

The firm also manufactures a family of process control products that combine the best of traditional distributed control technology with new, intelligent telemetry (telecontrol) techniques. Included is the Signature® line of electronic transmitters to meet the demands of today's process control applications with accurate and reliable measurement of flow, liquid level, temperature, pressure, and differential pressure.

In addition, Bristol Babcock is recognized as a leader in the production of instrumentation systems with its Network 3000 family, which allows computers to collect and distribute data, perform sophisticated man/machine interface functions, and excute supervisory control tasks. One of the most dramatic examples of this is the system that controls the Living Seas Pavilion at EPCOT Center, regulating the water temperature, chemical balance, and other factors in the aquarium.

Another example of the application of Bristol Babcock technology is the system in use on the American Natural Resource Gas Pipeline that runs from Detroit, Michigan, to Texas. It has some 23 compressor stations, all completely automated and supervised by an operator sitting on the eighteenth floor of the Renaissance Center in Detroit.

At Bristol Babcock, quality is designed into the products. The company's quality-assurance engineers work closely with its design engineers to create products among the most reliable on the market. The firm incorporates state-of-the-art automation technologies in the manufacturing, testing, and the inspection areas.

Meeting standards as tough as the military's, the company's quality-assurance program delivers products that have been built, inspected, and tested to meet a quality that well exceeds the process control industry standard, making Bristol Babcock Inc. the measure of the industry.

A view of one phase of the assembly of Bristol Babcock's Signature® line.

TIMEX

"Timex—It takes a lickin' and keeps on tickin'." This famous slogan, spoken assertively by John Cameron Swayze in commercials throughout the late 1950s and 1960s, describes not only a product, but an entire company. Just about everyone, it seems, has owned and sworn by a Timex watch, always known for durability and affordability.

Timex is a direct descendant of the Waterbury Clock Company, founded in 1857—one of many companies in an area that produced millions of clocks. Waterbury Clock Company was one of the largest man-

ABOVE: The Timex Doubles line for ladies wraps twice around the wrist, giving the watches more importance as a fashion accessory.

LEFT: The Timex Carriage Collection, an elegantly styled all-quartz watch collection for men.

ufacturers, and Timex is today the only firm in the Naugatuck Valley that successfully transitioned to watches.

Waterbury Clock Company clocks are eagerly sought by antique aficionados, as is its first watch—the "turnip" pocket watch, named for its appearance. During the early 1900s the company produced pocket watches under the Ingersoll brand name, naming the one-dollar timepiece the Ingersoll Yankee. It gained such great popularity that it became known as "the watch that made the dollar famous."

With the beginning of World War I, there were new demands for timepiece design. Artillery gunners needed an easy way to calculate and read time while still being able to work the guns. Thus, the wristwatch was born, with Waterbury Clock Company one of the first manufacturers. Following the war an agreement was reached with Walt Disney, resulting in the first million-dollar watch line that featured Mickey Mouse. Other early

The Timex Ironman Triathlon is America's best-selling watch of any type or brand.

timepieces starred Betty Boop, Tom Mix, and Gene Autry.

It wasn't until 1951 that the Timex brand name was introduced. By replacing jewels with long-wearing bearings, a new movement was developed, far less expensive than those in the existing Swiss watches, yet more durable and easier to produce. To prove that the inexpensive watches were well made, Timex produced live television commercials featuring news commentator John Cameron Swayze, the most credible spokesperson of his time. Swayze put the watches through a variety of torture tests, and at the end of each commercial, held the ticking Timex up to the camera lens and proclaimed, "Timex—It takes a lickin' and keeps on tickin'." The American public was impressed, and by 1960 Timex was the largest-selling watch in the country.

The 1970s proved to be the most tumultuous period in the company's 130-year history. New technology in the form of electronic digital watches and quartz analog watches was developing rapidly, making the Timex mechanical watch production facilities close to obsolete. Competition from American and foreign companies increased. Few domestic watch companies survived the technology change required to stay in business, but the Timex comeback was

successful, and eventually, all factories were converted to manufacture and assemble electronic products.

Whether a watch is multifunctional or simply tells the time, design is a top priority at Timex. In the early 1980s Timex established design studios in both Waterbury and France, employing a staff of professional industrial designers. The innovative design team has come up with a variety of fresh looks for the watch market, among them the Timex BBB line of classic fashion watches for women, con-

Early Timex character watches are popular collectors' items today.

stantly updated with new styles. For men, the Timex Carriage Collection offers a variety of fashion looks at an affordable price.

The leading producer of watches in the United States, Timex is the only domestic company to produce a full line of watches, 500 styles in all. In addition to the fashion lines, specialized sport watches have also become an exciting segment, gaining nationwide media coverage.

The Ironman Triathlon, the best-selling watch of any kind in America, is named after the grueling endurance event in Hawaii. It features rugged good looks and functions important to athletes who run, bike, and swim. The Timex Victory watch, designed specifically for sail racing, includes a racing countdown timer. A tack ratio

computer allows the racer to make a practice run to determine the final approach—a function previously performed only by an on-board computer. Other unique sport watches include the Timex Ski-athlon watch, which offers such features as a thermometer and stretch strap for wearing over a parka, and the Timex Aerobix, the first watch designed expressly for aerobic exercise.

In addition to sport and fashion watches, recent Timex innovations include watches with dials that light up brightly at the push of a button. Called Nightwatch, the concept is especially practical for people who work in low-light situations. PictureTime watches, produced in conjunction with Eastman Kodak Company, are customized with personal photographs on the dials.

Today Timex looks forward to the future, proud of its leadership position in the watch industry, built on a heritage of quality, value, and innovative design.

BUELL INDUSTRIES, INC.

In the 1930s and 1940s barley, hops, and malt were brewed in Waterbury and sold under the label Red Fox Beer. The advertising slogan for the local beer proclaimed that it was "Just what you've been hunting for."

Largay Brewery was the brainchild of George H. Largay, Sr., a poor farm boy who parlayed his grammar-school education into a career filled with savvy and ingenuity, beginning in the business when a friend offered him $1.50 to help him unload a carload of coal at a brewery.

made an investment of $22,000 and bought four headers. A strike at the Scovill Manufacturing Co. provided a source of skilled mechanics who were willing to work part time for the fledgling company. Al Schuerlein, a Largay family employee since 1930, also joined the firm and continued until his retirement in 1976.

First-year sales totaled $52,000 and a substantial loss. The company Christmas party was held with six people in one booth at Diorio's Restaurant. Thoughts of disbanding the operation were

ABOVE: John A. Largay founded the forerunner of today's Buell Industries, Inc., and served as its chief executive officer until his death in 1977.

LEFT: The old, historic Largay Brewery building where the original fastener company, the Connecticut Screw and Rivet Company, began in 1950.

Red Fox was brewed in Waterbury until 1948. Its distinctive red can found its way around the world with U.S. soldiers in World War II. By 1948 the strong marketing organizations of the big national brewers began to overwhelm the small local operators. Seven hundred and fifty breweries in the United States in 1937 became 230 by 1947. Faced with difficult odds, George Largay sold his brewing business to Jacob Ruppert Brewery of New York in 1948.

Using the old brewery building as a base, George's son, John A. Largay, started a fastener company— the Connecticut Screw and Rivet Company in 1950. In partnership with Andrew Connolly, Largay

quickly stifled by George Largay, who insisted his son continue. The firm was able, in 1952, to become a trial site for new equipment produced by the Waterbury Farrel company. This allowed the organization to become a competitive force in the marketplace.

In 1953 Largay joined forces with Russell Knecht, a knowledgeable sales representative from Detroit who introduced the company to the automotive business. In 1955 the company name was changed to Anchor Fasteners, and sales grew rapidly. Dix Becker, a genius engineer educated at MIT, joined the firm in 1958 and developed a series of innovative stamped products that fueled

Anchor's growth.

By 1960 John's brother Vincent joined the company and started its Bedford Heights, Ohio, operation. By this time, Anchor had outgrown the old brewery building, and a new plant was constructed on 13 acres of land on Huntingdon Avenue. The original 70,000 square feet has today grown to 220,000.

In 1962 Anchor merged with Buell Industries and became listed on the American Stock Exchange. The first cash dividend of 10 cents per share was paid in 1968. Today the company has more than 1,000 shareholders, including 20 percent of its 750 employees.

In 1971 Buell bought a portion of the discontinued eyelet business of Anaconda American Brass. In addition, three small eyelet companies were purchased and became the Highland Manufacturing division. Ray Alvey, then head of his own company, joined forces with Buell and provided much of the technical expertise needed to succeed

cessed there along with specialty Swedish ball bearing wire. The Ohio fastener plant has become an assembly and welding center producing specialty components such as air bag sensor housings. Future growth will come from patented products such as anti-cross threading fasteners and special body mount parts. Each year Buell produces more than 2 billion components for a variety of industries.

The Largay family no longer produces beer. But the company they guide, Buell Industries, makes its mark on the industrial landscape of America, providing necessary components that help keep the country on the move.

LEFT: Anchor Fasteners, a division of Buell Industries, Inc., manufactures products for the automotive industry at both its Waterbury (shown here) and Bedford Heights, Ohio, plants.

BELOW: The Highland Manufacturing division in Waterbury exports its products to 15 countries in every corner of the globe.

in this traditional business. George Largay's grandson, George, also joined this division.

Today the Highland Manufacturing division is viewed as a world leader in deep drawing quality and technology. A commitment to statistical process control, remanufactured equipment, and well-trained and motivated people has resulted in a corporation that exports its products to 15 countries in every portion of the globe.

In 1977 John Largay died. He left a successful company with $40 million in sales and 750 devoted and saddened employees. His commitment to people and the entrepreneurial spirit will be long remembered. Vincent Largay succeeded him as chief executive officer.

The 1980s saw annual sales grow to $90 million. A wire annealing and processing facility in Ohio has enjoyed great success. All the wire for Ford spark plugs is pro-

KEELER & LONG, INC.

Henry L. Long, Sr. (1897-1988), founded Keeler & Long, Inc., in 1928 in Waterbury to produce specialized paint products. One of these specialized paints was a light-sensitive varnish used in a process by the Scovill Manufacturing Company to etch designs on cosmetic containers and other brass products. This led to the development of Wipe-In Kolors used to decorate numbers, letters, and designs molded into metal or plastic items. This product is still in use today in the appliance, automobile, space, computer, and high-technology fields.

A nuclear power plant's turbine room floors, walls, structures, and equipment are painted with Keeler & Long epoxy, urethane, and silicone/alkyd paints.

The company grew in Waterbury from 1928 to 1973, when it relocated to Watertown into a new manufacturing plant, laboratory, and office facility. This change also involved passing the company management to the second generation: Henry Jr., William, and David Long.

Keeler & Long, Inc., became a leader in anticorrosive paints to protect steel exposed to weathering. The electric and gas utility industry provided the market potential, with structures, plants, tanks, and facilities that require protection from the corrosive elements of wind, water, and chemicals of an industrial environment.

Paints and coatings were developed to reduce maintenance costs

and maximize protective life. The 4400 Series, a single-coat primer/finish, was developed in 1955 to protect galvanized transmission towers and substation structures. It is used extensively by electric utility companies nationwide, and is the only product of its kind that protects for 20 or more years.

The 1960s brought forth huge construction projects by the utilities. Nuclear power, natural gas, hydroelectric, and fossil power plants required enormous quantities of paints and coatings. New paint technology was needed to solve the problems associated with high temperature exposures, water immersion service, aesthetic appeal, nuclear safety, and environmental compatibility. A white primer uniquely met these challenges. This concept was introduced in 1962 as a new type of anticorrosive primer to protect steel. It provided improved performance, cost savings, and eliminated toxic ingredients.

The new manufacturing facility occupied in 1973 gave the company the means to handle new and greater business opportunity. Its products, especially for the nuclear

The exterior metal surfaces of Shea Stadium in New York City are coated with a specially formulated Mets blue.

industry, were licensed to be manufactured in Europe and the Far East. The Kolors trademark may be seen in Taiwan, Japan, Europe, and Africa, and if present negotiations are successful, may next be seen in the Soviet Union. The Long brothers went to Moscow in 1987 to further discuss the possible sale of paints to the Soviet nuclear industry.

Keeler & Long, Inc., will face change and new opportunities in the future. The third generation of family management is becoming established as the business continues to expand into additional industries in need of high-performance paints and coatings. Pulp and paper, petrochemical, transportation, and nuclear maintenance portend the future. It will be met with a commitment of products that meet the increasingly stringent requirements that protect people and their environment and maintain the highest level of performance.

ERICKSON METALS CORPORATION

In Detroit another car rolls off the line. At the cosmetic counter of a New York department store, a woman considers a popular perfume hosting a decorative metal cap. In a downtown Waterbury pharmacy, customers in the checkout line carry cans of breath freshener, eyebrow pencils, and safety razors. These are just a few of the many everyday uses of Erickson's metals. Leading manufacturers select Erickson's aluminum products for automotive parts, computer casings, cosmetics, parts for modern aircraft, hinges on wedding albums, screw assemblies for light bulbs, writing instruments, and hundreds of other uses. Worldwide, Erickson's high-quality products can be found throughout such diverse industries as automotive, high tech, consumer goods, and aerospace.

Founded in 1972 by Richard H. Erickson to serve quality-conscious eyelet industry customers, the company was originally located in Oakville. Throughout the 1970s the growing aluminum warehousing and distribution center expanded in and around Waterbury, an area historically known for its eyelet and metal stamping industries.

In 1984 Erickson Rolling Mills, a division of Erickson Metals Corporation, was established. It is a state-of-the-art rolling facility, employing the most modern technology for metals processing. The 45,000-square-foot Connecticut plant includes corporate headquarters and is located in the Cheshire Industrial Park. In the early 1980s full-line aluminum service centers were opened in Minnesota and Colorado, broadening the distribution capabilities to customers for flat sheet, plate, rod, bar, wire, and extruded products.

The firm's steady growth can be traced to its commitment to quality, superior customer service, and an efficient corporate structure that supports fast turnaround and clear communication at all levels.

Erickson Metals' modern 45,000-square-foot Connecticut facility is located in the scenic Cheshire Industrial Park.

Erickson Metals offers more than full-line distribution services. Its products are tailored to customers' needs and include custom rolling and shearing, precision slitting and sawing, and cut-to-length processing. Employing the latest equipment, Erickson is able to hold aluminum rolling tolerances far closer than commercial standards. When a customer needs aluminum coil, Erickson rolls to the exact specifications enabling the client to obtain a high-quality, uniform product. In the manufacturing process, this means reduced waste and minimal machine adjustment—a real benefit to Erickson customers.

Erickson offers a complete range of tempers, and its computer-controlled inert gas annealing furnaces produce consistent, stain-free materials with minimum surface oxides. Slitting is also performed to customers' close tolerance specifications, creating easy-to-handle, tightly wound coils with less surface damage and less scrap.

The company's commitment to supply the finest metal products is evident in its discriminating selection of raw materials, exacting labo-

Erickson's 25-inch Sendzimir Mill maintains precise control of the rolling process, issuing reports verifying computer gauge control from reroll stock to finished coil.

ratory testing done on premises, and extensive employee training to maintain quality standards.

As an additional service to its customers, Erickson Metals Corporation maintains a complete stock of aluminum products and its own trucking fleet. The firm's emphasis on quality and service has given it a competitive position in the international metals market.

TECH SYSTEMS, DIVISION OF DATRON INC.

On board a nuclear-class aircraft carrier, the planes find their mark, landing on the runway in the middle of the ocean. These floating airports are critical to U.S. defense and a strategic part of their firing systems is a product manufactured locally.

Various types of wave guide products to be used in radar and communications systems.

Inside an airplane, the bleeps of the radar system provide the pilot with vital information, thanks in part to a local company. Tech Systems of Thomaston, a division of Datron Inc., provides, among other things, a shipboard auxiliary power supplier for fire control and radio systems. The firm also manufactures microwave guides and components for aircraft radar systems.

Tech Systems is actually two companies in one. Precise Power Systems is a leading designer and manufacturer of power conversion

The motor generator used on a U.S. government guard ship for conversion of 60-Hertz ship's power to 400 Hertz to supply 400-Hertz power for the ship's instruments.

equipment and systems. Motors and generators of all AC and DC types are designed and built in house, as are precision, high-efficiency, high-performance drives for both industrial and military uses.

Precise Power was founded in 1913 in Stamford as the Electric Specialty Co. and relocated to its current site at 401 Watertown Road in 1964. Also at that location is its sister operation, Technicraft, one of the nation's leaders in the design and manufacture of microwave waveguide and related components for both military and commercial uses. One major use is for U.S. military aircraft radar systems, although Technicraft's marketing operation is international in scope and its products sold in virtually every country in the free world.

Technicraft's rigid and flexible wave guides are considered a standard in the industry, and the firm's craftsmanship and technical skills are widely recognized. Originally founded in the Waterbury area in 1947, the organization moved to its present site in 1964.

The two companies became known as Tech Systems in 1972.

Both sides of the business produce essentially the same product lines they have pursued since their founding, with an increasing emphasis on high technology. The firm is dedicated to the continued involvement of its current product lines, expanding within the framework of its existing technologies.

Through the years the company has received much recognition in the field. One of only perhaps five corporations of its kind in the United States, the firm also has achieved noteworthiness as the largest manufacturer of flexible wave guides.

Tech Systems is design and engineering driven, providing innovative, quality products—products that serve on the frontline of America's defense.

Business and Professions

Greater Waterbury's business and professional community brings a wealth of service, ability, and insight to the area.

Greater Waterbury Chamber of Commerce, 186

Waterbury Convention & Visitors Commission, 187

Centerbank, 188

Lenkowski, Lonergan & Co., 192

Bank of Waterbury, 194

Jaci Carroll Personnel Services, Inc., 196

Carmody & Torrance, 198

Gager, Henry & Narkis, 200

Waterbury Development Agency, 202

H.D. Segur, Inc., 204

Connecticut Bank and Trust Company (CBT), 206

Bank of Boston Connecticut, 207

Cipriano & Associates, 208

Photo by Jack McConnell

GREATER WATERBURY CHAMBER OF COMMERCE

The economic development and well-being of the area is not a spectator sport for the Greater Waterbury Chamber of Commerce. Throughout its 100 years of history, the chamber has been an active player. On the forefront of economic development in Waterbury and the other 12 member towns it represents, the chamber's efforts often translate into the creation of jobs and the improvement of the social and economic climate of the area.

In part through the efforts of the chamber, the area has been able to remain competitive as well as growing and prospering. When the large brass companies closed down their operations, the organization moved to fill the void, helping, among other things, to reactivate the Naugatuck Valley Development Corporation, which served as the city's agent developer to create the Waterbury Industrial Commons at the site of the "mile-long" plant, donated to the city by Chase Brass.

The Naugatuck Valley Development Corporation obtained some $5 million in federal and state loans and grants, and the project created some 700 jobs. The commons was roughly 60 percent developed when sold in 1986.

The NVDC also developed and sold the land for an emissions facility erected by United Technologies for the mandatory testing required by the state.

In essence, the strength of the Greater Waterbury Chamber of Commerce is to do things that no one person or group could do. It is, for example, involved in education, co-sponsoring a Partners in Education program with the Waterbury School System and Connecticut Light and Power. In this program businesses are matched with schools, providing them with resources to enhance the academic and social development of students.

The chamber also provides assistance to member municipalities through its loaned executive pro-

TOP: The Greater Waterbury Chamber of Commerce is preparing to celebrate its 100th anniversary in its new quarters at 83 Bank Street.

ABOVE: The Waterbury Symphony is just one of the member organizations promoted by the chamber.

RIGHT: The chamber's Economic Report *features statistics and facts that provide vital information for area businesses.*

gram. In the past, for example, it performed a managerial audit for Waterbury, an energy audit for Watertown, and a personnel survey for Woodbury.

The organization also publishes a series of economic reports stocked with statistics and facts that provide vital information for area businesses. Such information might deal with housing, major employers, economic development trends, and available financing programs.

The chamber is also active in governmental affairs as "the voice of business," working with local, state, and federal leaders on a bipartisan basis to promote issues that are in the interest of local business.

In addition, the association maintains its position as a friend to all, fielding calls from people vacationing in the area who want to

know what to bring for clothing, to people relocating to the area who want information on housing, to businesses wishing to obtain more information about expanding.

The chamber is very involved in the communities it serves, promoting its member organizations in the region. In Waterbury, for example, it promotes the Waterbury Symphony, whose offices are housed in the chamber's own offices, as well as numerous other organizations such as the United Way, the Mattatuck Museum, the Up on Waterbury Committee, and others.

As the Greater Waterbury Chamber of Commerce prepares to celebrate its 100th anniversary, it is fitting to note its relocation to 10,000 square feet of space at 83 Bank Street in the heart of downtown and the region. That is where it fulfills its function as the supporting arm of business in the communities it serves, which include Beacon Falls, Bethlehem, Cheshire, Middlebury, Naugatuck, Oxford, Prospect, Southbury, Thomaston, Waterbury, Watertown, Wolcott, and Woodbury.

WATERBURY CONVENTION & VISITORS COMMISSION

Rolling out the welcome mat to thousands of visitors each year, the Waterbury Convention & Visitors Commission serves as the city's grand host, building on a 300-year tradition of New England hospitality. At the crossroads of Routes 8 and 84, Waterbury receives thousands of guests each year from the motorists passing through to organized conventions involving hundreds of people.

The WCVC was created in 1982 by an act of the Connecticut General Assembly. Charged with promoting Waterbury's special charms and its enduring attractions, the commission receives its ordinary income from a percentage of the room sales tax collected in the city's hotels, motels, and bed-and-breakfast establishments.

Shrugging off its image as an "old mill town," Waterbury has reclaimed its time-honored spot as a center of culture and commerce for the region. The commission has played an active part in Waterbury's renaissance, supporting numerous organizations and community events that celebrate the life of the mind and the spirit. Waterbury's well-known Mattatuck Museum and its much-loved Symphony Orchestra are only two of the more prominent institutions to benefit from WCVC sponsorship. From small neighborhood fairs to

ABOVE: The oldest continuous fife and drum corps in the United States dates back to 1767. Still going strong with 57 members today, the participants have ranged from six to 70 years of age.

ABOVE RIGHT: The clock tower at the railroad station is a familiar landmark in Waterbury.

RIGHT: This part of the Mattatuck Museum's Brass Roots Exhibit is a display of handcrafted household tools used to produce food and clothing in early nineteenth-century preindustrial Waterbury.

the ambitious Homecoming '87, which involved thousands of the city's past and present residents, WCVC involvement has made a difference.

The commission also supports special events that give flair and sparkle to urban living, such as the regional celebration of the Bicentennial of the United States Constitution in 1987. WCVC coordinated the celebration attended by thousands, which included Roads to Liberty, featuring original copies of the Magna Carta and the Declaration of Independence. The WCVC has also sponsored lectures and concerts, organizing the entire concert series in 1988 dedicated to jazz greats and heroes of the blues.

Waterbury prides itself on being a community where the past is al-

ways present, a philosophy exemplified by the WCVC's popular new trackless trolley, which can be seen bustling natives and visitors around the city. An inviting symbol of the Brass City, the trolley harkens to an earlier era in the Naugatuck Valley when Waterbury was the heart of an industrial empire.

Remnants of that empire are everywhere to be found, and the commission encourages visitors to carefully examine Waterbury's precious legacy of days gone by, publishing a guide to the city that includes a popular self-guided walking tour of downtown, aptly called Legacy and Promise. Others may wish to stroll through Waterbury's two other designated historic districts, Hillside and Overlook, where the past century's captains of industry built their magnificent homes.

Working in close cooperation with the state's 18 other tourism districts, the Waterbury Visitors & Convention Commission can provide information from throughout Connecticut and much of New England. Visitors and residents alike are encouraged to stop by the WCVC offices.

CENTERBANK

Waterbury was a pleasant, if sleepy, village in 1850 with tree-lined, unpaved streets and a population of 5,137. Yet the years that followed brought a period of dramatic changes. Industries prospered, the town's first large office buildings were erected—some of which were three stories high—and a modern hotel was built.

Town officials shocked many thrifty citizens by appropriating the sum of $125 "for erecting and sustaining gas lights from Center Square to the railroad station." The opening of service on the Naugatuck Railroad was to break down the town's previous isolation from the rest of Connecticut. It was in this atmosphere that Centerbank

was established.

Prior to the nineteenth century Waterbury was predominantly an agricultural community. Little cash, and especially little "hard cash," was held by the average citizen. What silver coins a farmer might accumulate during a lifetime were saved and converted into spoons or other tableware by the local silversmith.

However, industrial development brought money into the community in previously unheard-of

Until the merger in 1933, Centerbank's downtown branch was the headquarters for the Dime Savings Bank.

quantities. Employees in those industries began to earn amounts that might, in a few months, equal a far greater sum than their farmer-parents had possessed in a lifetime. The company store, which had served a financial role by extending consumer credit to employees and residents, waned as retail establishments were attracted to the area.

Quality customer service has been the foundation of Centerbank's success for more than 138 years.

With this growth in population, industry, and retail trade, it soon became apparent that further progress would be seriously hampered without more sophisticated financial institutions.

One area resident who watched the development of Waterbury with great interest, and had a clear appreciation of the importance of a financial institution to the future of the town and its people, was attorney Frederick J. Kingsbury. A native of Waterbury, Kingsbury was a renowned legal and civic leader. He recognized the obvious need for a safe and convenient place where people could save a part of their income and wasted no time in satisfying that need.

In his autobiography he wrote, "I had an idea that it would be a good thing to have a mutual savings bank in Waterbury, and so I got a charter for one." This first mutual institution, Waterbury Savings Bank, was established in 1850 for the purpose of providing a safe and profitable means of investment. Waterbury's most prominent town leaders were chosen as the bank's directors.

Many of Kingsbury's friends did not share his confidence in the bank's future. "I remember," he wrote, "some of our directors saying we might live to see $100,000 in deposits—though I think no one believed it."

In 1853 Frederick Kingsbury ceased practicing law to devote himself exclusively to banking. He lived to see his faith in Waterbury justified. Twenty years after the bank was founded, deposits totaled $1.6 million, and in 1910 the total had reached $6 million.

In 1870 the city's population

Centerbank's SERVIS® automated teller machines provide customers with access to their money 24 hours per day.

was 13,106, more than double the 1850 figure. Factory payrolls had increased even more rapidly. The need for another financial institution was met by the establishment of Dime Savings Bank, Waterbury's second mutual savings bank. On January 1, 1874, deposits in Dime Savings Bank totaled $250,000 from more than 2,000 depositors.

In 1889 West Side Savings Bank was chartered. It prospered in Waterbury until the Great Depression of the 1930s, when depositors' concerns over the safety of their money caused them to with-

draw their funds in record amounts. While West Side Savings was a solid financial institution, its capital was invested in real estate loans and not easily accessible. Connecticut's banking commissioner, in hopes of saving West Side Savings Bank, ordered it be merged with Dime Savings Bank and Waterbury Savings Bank.

On August 1, 1933, the consolidation of these three banks was completed. This produced the fourth-largest savings bank in Connecticut, and the 70th largest in the country. The new institution retained the name "Waterbury Savings Bank," and moved into the Dime Savings office, located on the corner of North Main and Savings streets, where Centerbank's main office sits today.

Waterbury Savings Bank always maintained a reputation of fine service to the community it served. To thousands of individuals, its name was associated with a remarkable record of integrity, sound operation, and the protection of personal savings. By 1974, though, Waterbury Savings Bank had expanded to six diversified communities.

In order to reflect this broadened scope, an expanded product line that included such items as checking accounts and credit

Activities such as the United Way's local bed race are just one way that Centerbank shows its community spirit and pride.

cards, and rapidly developing changes in the financial industry, the Waterbury Savings Bank changed its name to The Banking Center in April 1974.

In October 1981 John P. Burke was elected president and chief executive officer. Under his guidance, The Banking Center merged with Woodbury Savings in 1983. This merger provided the bank with direct access to the rapidly developing, economically vital, and highly competitive trading area comprised of the towns of Woodbury, Southbury, and Bethlehem.

The bank's conversion to stock ownership was one of the biggest steps taken since its establishment. In order to fund its ambitious growth objective, The Banking Center converted from a mutual savings bank to a stock bank on August 13, 1986, with the issuance of more than 12 million shares of stock. With this conversion, more than $150 million in capital was raised, one of the largest offerings in New England savings bank history.

By 1988 it was recognized

Providing the funds for businesses to grow has helped Waterbury to grow.

that the name "The Banking Center" did not accurately represent the institution. The name had also become generic, with more than 35 firms and services identified nationally as using "banking center" in their names. After extensive research the name "Centerbank" was chosen.

Today Centerbank stands as the area's largest independent financial institution. While its headquarters remains in Waterbury, its branch network stretches along the I-84 corridor from Danbury to Southington. The bank's residential mortgage lending operation, Centerbank Mortgage Company, has offices in Connecticut, New York, New Jersey, Massachusetts, South Carolina, and Georgia. Realtech and Burgdorff Realtors, the bank's real estate brokerage subsidiaries, meet the needs of home buyers and sellers in Connecticut, New Jersey, and eastern Pennsylvania. An equipment leasing firm, Center Capital Corporation, serves New England.

As the largest financial institution headquartered in western Con-

necticut, Centerbank has had an enormous impact on the rebirth of Waterbury. Numerous commercial and residential construction projects throughout the area have been financed by the bank. Many of the cars on the highways and the home improvements down the block can be attributed to the

bank's creative financing options and its willingness to commit funding to the community. Yet, Centerbank's impact on Waterbury cannot be measured only by the money it lends.

Centerbank has continually demonstrated its unswerving corporate commitment to improving Waterbury, not only for its employees, but for its customers. Despite the bank's geographic diversification over the past decade, its heart remains in the Brass City.

A strong force in the city are the bank's employees, most of whom live in the Waterbury area. Each of these people has an individual stake in the resurgence of Waterbury, and are the bank's, and the city's, greatest assets. Their involvement with and contributions to numerous civic and cultural organizations is well documented. Centerbank supports their efforts through an extensive corporate giv-

Nicknamed "Roadies" because they spend so much time traveling, these consumer and residential mortgage loan originators will come to a client's home or business, any time of the day or night.

John P. Burke, president and chief executive officer of Centerbank.

ing program that specifically targets the needs of the community. All manners of contributions—time, money, services, materials, and personnel—are donated in an effort to better help Waterbury.

One organization that benefits from this concern is the United Way of the Central Naugatuck Valley. President John P. Burke was one of the developers of the local appeal and served as the campaign's first chairman. Each year since the fund's inception a member of Centerbank's upper management team has held a key role with the United Way. In addition, Centerbank employees routinely participate in the United Way's Loaned Executives program, bringing their expertise and knowledge to this most important community fund drive.

Yet Centerbank's commitment to Waterbury only starts with the annual United Way campaign. As an organization, the bank sup-

ports programs for hundreds of groups. The Anderson Boys Club, the Children's Community School, the YMCA, and Big Brothers/Big Sisters of Greater Waterbury are just a few of the groups that receive support. In addition, Centerbank's employees serve on the boards of many of these organizations and volunteer considerable personal time toward making them a success.

The city's cultural climate, another integral part of Waterbury's rebirth, is also critical to Centerbank. The Waterbury Symphony Pops Concert is sponsored annually by the bank, with many tickets donated to those who might not be able to otherwise at-

tend a live music performance. The summer concert series, the Waterbury Arts Festival, and art auctions to benefit area children have all been part of Centerbank's agenda.

Waterbury's people and industries are the reason for the city's newfound pride. The resurgence during the past decade has infected all who work and live there, resulting in a community spirit and concern that is unrivaled anywhere else in the state. Businesses, professional groups, service organizations, and individual residents, though, are not only the forces responsible for the rebirth of Waterbury, but ultimately, will be its beneficiaries. Centerbank takes great pride in knowing that it has had such a large part in the development of Waterbury's next great era.

Buying a house is one of the biggest decisions a couple will make in their lifetime. Centerbank has helped countless people achieve the dream of home ownership.

LENKOWSKI, LONERGAN & CO.

Lenkowski, Lonergan & Co., 141 East Main Street, the largest local CPA firm in Waterbury, is accountable—to its clients, to its peers, to itself.

"Account-ability" is the cornerstone of the company—founded in 1965 by Robert A. Lenkowski—that serves clients in Connecticut, Rhode Island, Massachusetts, and New York.

The firm, one of the first in the country to voluntarily enroll in the AICPA Peer Review Program, undergoes an intensive peer review once every three years. The CPA

LEFT: Tax department personnel and partners research and discuss a tax question.

BELOW: The four partners at the entrance to the office (from left): William M. Lonergan, CPA; Paul M. Scionti, CPA; Robert A. Lenkowski, CPA; and John R. Sullivan, CPA.

The staff attend an in-house continuing education seminar.

firm recently completed its third successful review, receiving an Unqualified Opinion—the highest recommendation for quality that the accounting profession has to offer.

Such achievements don't come lightly; they come by hard and honest work. "The most valuable assets are human resources," says Lenkowski. "We have a group of professionals and support people second to none, bringing honesty, integrity, ethics, enthusiasm, and technical capabilities—in that order—to everything they do."

The primary objective of the firm is to furnish its clients with the finest in professional services to meet ongoing needs in as timely a manner as possible. The company strives continuously for excellence and higher levels of service through a practice that adheres to professional standards and commands the respect of its colleagues. While the monetary rewards of professional practice are important, they are viewed as secondary to ethical conduct.

Lenkowski, Lonergan & Co. has developed expertise in various specialty areas, including the service sector, medical practices, and automotive dealerships. It also serves many companies in manufacturing, construction, wholesale, retail, and professional operations.

In addition to traditional services, which include auditing, financial statements, and tax return preparation, the firm offers a wide variety of management and advisory functions. It offers expertise in such areas as operations management, personnel flow charting, computer feasibility studies, cash flow, income projection, and real estate evaluation.

Whether it's a simple tax return, a sophisticated tax problem, or a real estate situation, the professionals at Lenkowski, Lonergan & Co. take a team approach. The team concept is the key to the firm's operation and is behind every-

thing it does.

The firm currently has a total staff of more than 30, including four partners. Lenkowski was joined by partners William M. Lonergan in 1967, John R. Sullivan in 1971, and Paul M. Scionti in 1987. The firm established its name as Lenkowski, Lonergan & Co. in 1971.

In order to serve clients better, the firm became a part of CPA Associates, Inc., an association of select, local, independent CPA firms with members in major cities throughout the United States, as well as international associates in seven countries abroad. Exacting professional requirements must be satisfied by firms admitted to CPA Associates, and periodic inspections of members are conducted to ensure the continuance of the highest standards.

This program offers the best of both worlds. Because Lenkowski, Lonergan & Co. maintains its autonomy, it can provide personal attention and continuity of service. On the other hand, the firm can offer clients services and benefits that are typically available only through national CPA firms, and without the overhead of a larger firm.

With more than 250 partners and 1,500 staff generating more than $100 million in fee income per year, the member firms of CPA Associates would constitute one of the largest CPA firms in the United States if they were to practice as a single unit. These resources are Len-

kowski, Lonergan & Co.'s resources.

CPA Associates facilitates the sharing of both ideas and expertise among member firms, thus helping members to improve the quality and profitability of their practices while enhancing client service. As a member, Lenkowski, Lonergan & Co. maintains its independence, but can tap into the collective expertise of CPA Associates. "We like to tell our clients we are serving them better through CPA Associates. Why CPA Associates? Because if we don't have the answer, one of the member firms will," Lenkowski says.

He also points out that partners and staff of his firm are able to sharpen their professional and management expertise at association seminars and programs, and then can apply the members' industry knowledge to client engagements.

Lenkowski, Lonergan & Co.'s affiliation with CPA Associates helps put it on the leading edge, partly because daily exchanges with associates constantly address a variety of client and professional concerns, thus the firm is able to gauge emerging trends in business, all with the goal of staying ahead of the changing needs of clients. "The principal objective of our firm," says Lenkowski, "is to perform outstanding service for clients."

BANK OF WATERBURY

Question: What happens when a group of community and business leaders, many of them entrepreneurs, get together to form a financial institution with strong community ties?

Answer: A real success story: Bank of Waterbury.

The commercial bank, which opened its doors on April 17, 1985, has carved a niche as an independent bank with a community per-spective, maintaining a strong posture in the mainstream of Waterbury.

In an era of mergers and acquisitions that would seem to make such a person as a "local banker" obsolete, Bank of Waterbury is a hands-on type of institution that is committed to those it serves. Bank of Waterbury, located at 255 Bank Street, is a full-service institution that utilizes its knowledge of the community and the people in it to provide for the financial requirements of individuals and businesses.

The small businessperson is one of the main focuses of the bank. These people, in whose ranks are very small manufacturers and mom-and-pop entrepreneurs, are often considered too small to receive very much personal attention at large institutions. All too often they find that the bigger banks simply have other priorities.

Such customers are considered a main priority at Bank of Wa-

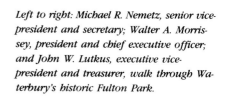

Left to right: Michael R. Nemetz, senior vice-president and secretary; Walter A. Morrissey, president and chief executive officer; and John W. Lutkus, executive vice-president and treasurer, walk through Waterbury's historic Fulton Park.

terbury. The bank realizes that, in many cases, small business owners need more than just the basics. They need the advice and expertise of a knowledgeable financial person, which they would generally be unable to obtain to a great enough degree from a larger bank.

"It all boils down to service," according to Bank of Waterbury president Walter A. Morrissey. "In a small community bank such as ours, service is the difference. Everyone becomes involved. Even top management is able to become immersed in the process of meeting the individual needs of customers."

Obviously this difference has proved successful for Bank of Waterbury, which accrued approximately $50 million in total assets in its first three years, and is growing at an estimated 15 to 20 percent annual rate.

"We believe this estimate for future years is realistic as this marketplace continues to expand," says Morrissey. "We feel very strongly about the economic progress of Waterbury and that the progress will continue. It is a very fine place to do business."

Bank of Waterbury's commitment to the Brass City expanded in 1988 with the addition of its first branch in the east end of the city, at 2154 East Main Street. The bank intends to establish additional branches on a selective basis in the upcoming years, in order to provide convenience to its customers.

And as the ground is broken for each new branch, it is another dream come true for the bank's organizers, many of whom operated businesses in Waterbury, and who, according to Morrissey, "are extremely interested in the development of the community. When they first began meeting in August 1983, they had a vision that they realized would require many complicated steps to turn into reality."

Forming a bank is a lengthy process, requiring reams of paperwork and volumes of procedures. But the individuals were committed to the task, believing there was not only a need but also a strong demand for a community-based commercial bank. They were motivated by the fact that the last of the city's independent commercial banks had just been acquired, leaving what they considered to be a gaping hole in the community.

Since 1983 they were busy compiling paperwork and attending hearings. A temporary charter, granted in December of that year, allowed them to begin forming the bank by making a formal application to both the state and the FDIC (Federal Deposit Insurance

Corporation), and to raise capital.

The organizers developed an offering statement, with the intention of selling up to 750,000 shares of stock during the period from June to December 1984. Incredibly, some 300,000 shares were sold in the first two months, and the balance was sold in the latter four months. The bank's shareholders are a broad-based, community-oriented group of about 1,000 individuals, with about 84 percent of the shareholders living in the Waterbury area.

In March 1985 the FDIC insurance was approved, and the bank opened about one month later.

The institution has experienced steady growth throughout the course of its short history, and, according to Morrissey, "The expertise of both management and the bank's board members serves as a referral service for new business. And the growth of the institution is assured by virtue of the fact that these individuals continuously improve their knowledge of the community and the needs of borrowers and depositors in the area."

Whether it's free checking accounts for small businesses, or a simple passbook savings account, Bank of Waterbury is dedicated to providing the same types of products of a larger bank. "So often people can fall through the cracks at larger banks," says Morrissey. "This is a prospect that is not at all appealing to customers, and our mission is to see it does not happen here. Bank of Waterbury is here to serve the community. We are of Waterbury, by Waterbury, for Waterbury."

Many Bank of Waterbury employees are involved in various community activities, and the board of directors is composed of leading citizens who are active in many organizations. "Our posture," says Morrissey, "is one of strong community service with a commitment to maintaining that high level of involvement."

Bank of Waterbury's spacious main office at 255 Bank Street.

JACI CARROLL PERSONNEL SERVICES, INC.

Jaci Carroll Personnel Services, Inc., is the area's largest locally owned and managed temporary help company. The firm's headquarters on Leavenworth Street in downtown Waterbury is comprised of more than 8,000 square feet of newly renovated office space. Two branch offices are located in Torrington and Southbury. Other branches are in the planning stages.

Jaci Carroll, president and founder of Jaci Carroll Personnel Services, Inc.

Jaci Carroll Personnel Services, Inc., was founded in 1976 by its president, Jaci Carroll, a lifelong resident of Waterbury and a veteran in the temporary help industry. Since its inception the firm has played an active, vital role in the economic development of the greater

Waterbury area. Consistent parallel patterns appear as one traces the growth of this local company, the growth of the temporary help industry as a whole, and the growth of the area's business milieu.

Combining a keen sense of business with years of experience in an industry that was still young, Jaci Carroll opened her company in a small, one-room, second-floor office on Bank Street in February 1976. With two employees, two desks, and a small loan, the business was born.

Jaci quickly introduced new ideas in personnel staffing and management. Businesses that formerly only purchased temporary help for vacation fill-ins began to plan ahead, purchasing temporary help for peak work loads and special projects. Job orders kept coming. The

temporary help service and the company's Permanent Placement Agency kept growing.

In 1979 Jaci Carroll Personnel Services moved to its present location at 37 Leavenworth Street. That same year a branch office was opened in Torrington. In 1987, to accommodate further growth, the company assumed an additional 3,000 square feet of available space at the same location.

Offering businesses the most highly qualified temporary workers has always been a challenge. Jaci Carroll Personnel Services maintains a stringent testing program. With more space available, the company implemented a new facet of its business plan. It opened the Jaci Carroll P.C. Training Center. There, in a fully equipped high-tech classroom, temporary workers are able to learn the latest in current PC business software program applications. No simulators are used. Two full-time instructors supervise hands-on experience on actual hardware and software. Investment in this training center has allowed the firm to continually send qualified workers into the work force even when Connecticut's low unemployment rate has made this a most difficult task.

Early in 1989, as a response to the growing number of businesses needing temporary help in the Waterbury/Danbury corridor, Jaci Carroll Personnel Services opened another branch office in Southbury. The full-service office provides added convenience for temporary workers and businesses in that market area.

To better understand the temporary help industry and to bring innovative staffing trends into the greater Waterbury market area, Jaci Carroll has always maintained a high profile on a national level. When she joined the National Association of Temporary Services (NATS) in 1976, there were only 200 member firms. Her leadership in the industry was soon recognized, and she was nominated to var-

Katherine Hanratty, vice-president (right), and staff discuss the new software programs currently being taught in the Jaci Carroll P.C. Training Center.

ious positions on the executive board. In 1987 she was elected president of NATS. Jaci became the national spokesman for the organization, which had grown to include more than 900 member companies. These businesses represent more than 85 percent of the total sales in an industry that generated more than $9.9 billion in payroll dollars in 1988.

Jaci Carroll Personnel Services is also a member of IOSI (The Independent Office Services Institute). IOSI is a national network of independently owned and operated temporary help services. Membership is by invitation only and is typically offered to the best/largest independently owned company in a market area. Founded in 1962, IOSI's primary purpose is to pro-

vide a forum for the free exchange of ideas affecting the operation of a temporary help service.

The IOSI network has affiliate offices in 73 market areas nationwide, with locations in California, Colorado, Connecticut, Florida, Illinois, Iowa, Kansas, Maryland, Massachusetts, Michigan, Minnesota, New York, Ohio, Oklahoma, Oregon, South Carolina, Texas, Utah, Virginia, Washington, D.C., and Puerto Rico.

Eileen Hanratty, operations manager (standing), reviews a temporary assignment with a personnel counselor and an applicant.

The company's strong sense of what is occurring on a national level is coupled with a deep commitment to the local community. Jaci and members of the staff serve on numerous boards of business and civic organizations. In 1989 Carroll assumed the position of chairman of the Greater Waterbury Area Chamber of Commerce, a vital organization working for thousands of businesses in Waterbury and 13 surrounding towns.

Since its beginning in 1976 Jaci Carroll Personnel Services has literally placed hundreds of thousands of people into the work force. Thirty full-time employees

now staff day-to-day operations at three locations. The staff includes bilingual employee counselors able to serve Waterbury's growing Hispanic population. The firm's annual sales are well into the multimillion-dollar figures.

Jaci Carroll Personnel Services, Inc., has played a major role in the revitalization of the greater Waterbury area's business climate. The guiding force behind the company's strong growth has been its

president and founder, Jaci Carroll. The words used at a recent ceremony at which Jaci Carroll received a Humanitarian Service Award best summarize the value and extent of her commitment to the local community: "Jaci has helped shape the economic, social, and cultural landscape of our community and is one of the key players in the resurgence of the central Naugatuck Valley in recent years."

CARMODY & TORRANCE

The year was 1861. The United States introduced the first passport system. Wagner's *Tannhauser* opened in Paris and caused a scandal. Mrs. Beaton came out with her *Book of Household Management*. And Charles Dickens wrote *Great Expectations*.

Meanwhile, in Waterbury, the forerunner of the Waterbury law firm of Carmody & Torrance had come into being with a solid legal ethic that was to take it toward the twenty-first century.

At that time the original attorney could hardly know that the firm he had founded would survive him by many years, growing many times over in size until today, when it has about 45 lawyers, includ-

The offices of Carmody & Torrance are at 50 Leavenworth Street, a stately old building that has been completely renovated to maintain its charm while updating its looks.

ing 19 partners, and law offices in Waterbury and New Haven.

Through the years the firm has experienced many changes and many partnerships. The earliest written evidence of a law partnership involving a Carmody or a Torrance is a listing in the 1902 city directory for the law firm of Burpee & Carmody, at 36 North Main Street. Lucien F. Burpee, 20 years senior to Terrence Carmody, left the firm after five years when he was appointed judge of the Superior Court.

At this point Mr. Carmody continued practicing law as a sole practitioner for almost six years, during which time he moved his office to 111 West Main Street, a building that today is commonly referred to as the Lilley Building. This was to remain the home of all subsequent Carmody & Torrance partnerships for nearly 60 years.

The firm continued to expand. In 1921 Mr. Carmody received a prestigious appointment to the position of state's attorney which he maintained for almost 10 years.

Over the years the firm has operated under many names, but has conducted the practice of law under its present name since 1955. In June 1979 it moved to its current location at 50 Leavenworth Street, originally the home of R.F. Griggs & Company, and later of First Federal Savings and Loan. The stately old building was completely renovated, maintaining its charm

The team approach practiced by the firm assures that a client's needs are promptly and effectively met.

while updating its look.

The firm practices general law with an orientation toward litigation and business clients. "Good, solid legal work" is the hallmark of the firm, and the philosophy is that "the best way to succeed as a law firm is to do good work."

Essentially, Carmody & Torrance provides legal services to individuals, businesses, and financial institutions based in Connecticut or engaged in transactions in Connecticut. Although clients are considered clients of the firm rather than of any particular attorney, one attorney generally maintains responsibility to oversee or direct specific cases and, when necessary, to put together a group representing differ-

ent specialties. This team approach helps ensure that clients' needs are met promptly and effectively.

The trend at Carmody & Torrance is to hire lawyers who are primarily law school honors graduates. Many of its attorneys have served on Law Review, and they represent a diverse group of top law schools. Many of Carmody & Torrance's attorneys serve on committees of both the Connecti-

cut Bar and the American Bar associations, and several are involved in various aspects of legal education.

About one-half of the firm's lawyers are office practitioners, concentrating in client counseling and transactional work, while the rest specialize in litigation. The former group is divided into specialized practice groups, including corporate/commercial, tax and estate planning, real estate, and labor. Attorneys within each group also work jointly with attorneys in other practice groups on matters related to their special subject areas.

The corporate/commercial group acts as general counsel and also handles specific transactions when requested by a client. Such transactions include mergers, acquisitions, divestitures, recapitalizations, and private placements. This group also handles a large variety

of matters pertaining to the Uniform Commercial Code. The firm's labor group represents the management of many profit and nonprofit organizations in all aspects of the employment relationship, including union relations, facility relocation and close downs, employee compensation and benefits, employment discrimination, safety and health, employment contracts, and other personnel issues. Where appropriate, the members of the labor group often rely on the expertise of the firm's corporate and litigation attorneys.

The tax and estate planning group handles a wide variety of federal and state tax matters, prepares and advises clients on employee benefit plans, and appears before various courts and administrative agencies on litigated matters. This group also counsels individuals on estate planning and advises fiduciaries and beneficiaries regarding estate probate and tax matters.

The firm's real estate group is involved with a large variety of commercial and industrial real estate functions, including sales and acquisitions, condominium projects, land-use planning, and land development.

Carmody & Torrance maintains an extensive litigation practice at all levels of the federal and state courts and before various administrative agencies, in matters ranging from medical malpractice to product liability to securities litigation.

The firm also has a long and successful history of representing individuals injured through the negligent conduct of others, and enjoys a statewide reputation in this area.

But whether it's a wrongful death suit or a labor dispute, the objective is the same. Carmody & Torrance is committed to the creed that client satisfaction is its stock in trade, and it strives to serve clients' needs promptly and efficiently with the highest quality of legal services.

GAGER, HENRY & NARKIS

The reception and conference area at the main office of Gager, Henry & Narkis.

In 1917 a young man named William Gager opened a law firm in Waterbury. Little did Gager know that the firm he founded that year would grow to include more than 50 lawyers and paralegals, becomming a law firm well known in the region, representing a large number of individual, corporate, and financial clients that includes many of the area's largest employers.

William Gager was born in Derby on March 20, 1892. His father, Edwin Baker Gager, later achieved fame as a justice of the Supreme Court of Connecticut.

The young Gager attended Yale Law School, graduating Magna Cum Laude in 1916. After practicing in New Haven, he settled in Waterbury, where he was in active practice—excluding a period of military service in World War I—for a half-decade.

His solid character and commitment to excellence and service in the practice of law set the tone for the modern-day firm. Today GH&N is a full-service law firm with special emphasis on services needed by businesses.

The firm is organized into seven departments. The Corporate Department performs services for business clients that include corporate and partnership law, securities and trade regulations, mergers and

A corporate acquisition team prepares for a merger transaction.

Don Henry at work on an estate settlement matter.

acquisitions, labor and employment, environmental, computer law, and commercial and business transactions.

The Banking Department is devoted to all aspects of federal and state banking laws and regulations. Included among Gager, Henry & Narkis clients are two of the state's largest banks, in addition to numerous smaller institutions.

The Real Estate and Lending Department provides services that include residential closings, commercial leases, real estate partnerships and syndications, condominium developments, subdivisions, environmental, zoning, and other land-use control matters.

The work of the Litigation Department involves handling a broad range of litigation and environmental matters, including representation of both plaintiffs and defendants, performing both trial and appellate work in virtually all areas other than criminal law.

Attorneys in the Trusts, Estates, and Probate Department engage in all aspects of estate planning and render advice concerning estate, inheritance, and gift taxation, as well as the income taxation of estates and trusts. They also handle all aspects of trust and estate administration.

The Tax Department includes all aspects of individual and business taxation, a large employee benefit plan practice, and tax-exempt organizations.

Finally, the Intellectual Property Department represents the firm's clients in all aspects of intellectual property law, including patents, trademarks, copyrights, trade secrets, and unfair competition.

Gager, Henry & Narkis also contributes its services to a variety of community organizations. The firm encourages employee involvement on the local level, and many of its attorneys are active on the boards of many charitable, community, and other such organizations. The firm also participates in the Connecticut Pro Bono Program.

Through the years the tone established by William Gager has been maintained. While he passed away in 1967, he is survived by named partners Donald W. Henry and Robert J. Narkis.

The firm's principal office is in Waterbury, at One Exchange Place, and it also maintains offices in Danbury, Sharon, and Southbury.

Gager, Henry & Narkis is confident that the rapid development and economic expansion of Waterbury will continue, and that prosperity in the business community will provide an excellent base for the continued growth of the firm.

State-of-the-art computers support the practice of law at Gager, Henry & Narkis.

WATERBURY DEVELOPMENT AGENCY

Behind every great city there are people, individuals of vision who not only see what is, but what can be. Such people are the lifeblood of the Waterbury Development Agency, an agency with a mission to create jobs, expand the tax base, and stimulate the economic growth of Waterbury.

As the city leaves the Brass Age and enters the era of high technology, the Waterbury Development Agency is the catalyst behind much of this growth, working in the background putting together prime parcels of land to attract developers, promoting the image of the city, and providing incentives, in certain cases, for the relocation of businesses into Waterbury.

The agency has achieved much in recent years, including the creation of some 1.5 million square

Work is under way on the downtown Buckingham Square redevelopment project consisting of a 206-room Crowne Plaza Hotel, a 650-car parking garage, and 10,000 square feet of new and renovated office space. The $26-million project highlights the renaissance of Waterbury.

feet of industrial space and more than 3,500 jobs through the development of three industrial parks— Reidville Industrial Park, Captain Neville Drive, and the Cherry Street Mini Industrial Park.

The agency's economic emphasis was broadened with the creation of an Enterprise Zone in 1987, truly the agency's centerpiece of economic development. The Enterprise Zone includes some 1,200 acres of designated land that parallels the Route 8 corridor from the Naugatuck to the Watertown town lines and provides incentives for manufacturing, commercial, and retail firms that relocate there or for existing facilities that expand operations. It also provides incentives for home or apartment building owners who make certain improvements.

Also on the industrial front, New Waterbury, the former home of Century Brass, a complex comprised of 90 buildings with more than 2.7 million square feet, came to fruition with the involvement of the Waterbury Development Agency.

In order to ensure continued business interest in Waterbury, the agency has developed and maintains a computerized property tracking system that keeps up-to-date information on tap about industrial,

The central Green of Waterbury, completely revitalized in the early 1980s, forms the backdrop and centerpiece for continued revitalization efforts that have created a harmonious architectural blend of the old and the new.

commercial, and retail properties, in essence acting in the capacity of a nonprofit broker.

The agency has also concentrated much effort in the development of the downtown area. As new buildings are erected, an artful blend of old and new merge to create an aesthetically pleasing city. While formalized efforts began more than two decades ago with the agency's creation of The Central Business District Urban Renewal Project, the revitalization of the central area continues with renewed vitality, paving the way for a harmonious relationship of building with landscape, of the modern with the traditional.

Preserving Waterbury landmarks is indeed a main thrust of the agency. It was highly instrumental, for example, in achieving the des-

ignation of the downtown historic district. One of the group's notable accomplishments in this vein is the part it played in saving Drescher's Restaurant, a longtime Waterbury landmark; the agency helped find a new owner for the building, which was scheduled for demolition. Waterburians will fondly recall the snail-paced relocation of the building to its present site on Leavenworth Avenue, a journey that took almost eight months to accomplish, with the building on wheels inching its way several blocks.

In 1988 the agency oversaw the $7-million improvement project that revitalized the eastern section of the central business district, fashioning the charm of a Victorian setting, with redbrick streets and sidewalks, 1920 look-alike gaslights, and Victorian-style park benches.

The piece de resistance of the area will be the transformation of the Palace Theatre into a renovated, $10.5-million arts center, a private project being undertaken by Domenic Temporale. Plans include a fully renovated theater, a Victorian restaurant, office space, spe-

cialty shops, and a continental sidewalk cafe, along with the Temporale Foundation for the Performing Arts.

The agency has also devoted much of its efforts to the development of the new Buckingham Square, with its 206-room Crowne Plaza hotel, a 57,000-square-foot office building, a 650-space parking garage, and the incorporation and renovation of four historic buildings.

On the drawing board is the 1.5-million-square-foot shopping mall in the south end, which represents a $200-million development that will accommodate 3,000 full-time and 1,500 part-time employees, and add $4 million to the city's tax base.

The Waterbury Development Agency's efforts have helped provide the necessary catalyst for the creation of many other such projects by area developers, including the construction and renovation of the Mattatuck Museum, the expansion and renovation of the Bank of Boston Connecticut, and the creation of One Exchange Place.

The major role of the agency is to serve as a catalyst, to keep making things happen in Waterbury. This goal is accomplished in several different ways. Making land acquisitions for the purpose of resale to developers for projects, typically under market value, is but one way. In some cases parcels are pieced together and the land is initially developed by the agency; in other cases it is sold "as is."

In addition to fostering the environment for new development, the agency has an extensive outreach program, formulating media campaigns to show Waterbury's "new face" to the world. While the nature of the city has changed from its mill town image of past decades, the Waterbury Development Agency wants to make sure that it is recognized as the thriving city that it is—a great place to live and work.

H.D. SEGUR, INC.

In 100 years man has advanced from the horse and buggy to space flight, from country stores to super malls. But sometimes, the more things change, the more things stay the same.

Take H.D. Segur, Inc., one of Connecticut's largest independent insurance agencies. Since 1890 the firm has provided the same high quality of service to its clients, individualized service that all too often seems to have gone out of style in today's world.

At the same time the firm has exhibited a great degree of adaptability. While most companies established before the turn of the century are mere memories, H.D. Segur has grown to become a recognized leader in the state. What set H.D. Segur apart from the beginning was its ability to evolve with conditions, developing ways to solve new problems while maintaining a strong emphasis on client advocacy.

H.D. Segur serves the client first. The basis of the company's

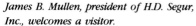

James B. Mullen, president of H.D. Segur, Inc., welcomes a visitor.

Determining a client's insurance needs is part of the review process.

first century of success is its ability to match each client with the best coverage at the fairest available price. Each Segur protection program is prepared with the client's input, based on such factors as its type of business, its situation in the marketplace, the varieties of exposure, and the degree to which the client's affairs are subject to change.

Segur people regularly confer with clients about proposed changes in their personal or business life, with an eye to minimizing possible future risk. This constant concern for preventing problems before they arise is a Segur standard. How a business client, for example, designs, manufactures, and distributes its products can have a significant impact on its insurance program. Segur personnel seek to keep abreast of changes in the law and regulations to provide invaluable advice on how insurance will affect operations—or how operations will affect insurance.

And while Segur places its primary emphasis on servicing clients, the company's established position in the Waterbury community extends to its relationships with the major insurance companies it represents. These include the Travelers, the Hartford, Crum and Forster, Crown Life, Blue Cross/Blue Shield, and many others. Through the development of solid relationships with such carriers, Segur can give priority to client needs.

The mission of H.D. Segur as a growing multiline regional agency is to offer a balance of professional, sophisticated insurance and financial services to commercial and personal clients, while emphasizing the best interest of its customers, as well as opportunity for growth and security for its employees and continued profitability.

The company, which moved to its present location at 255 Bank Street in 1988, has a dedicated staff of professionals with the experience, talent, and knowledge to keep abreast of the rapidly changing insurance industry. These experts know the business inside and out, top to bottom.

In today's world insurance requirements are increasingly complex. In 1890 there was no workers' compensation, no OSHA, no ICC, no FTC. Product liability and environmental protection were still unknown. The needs of the customers were simpler, more straightforward.

Over the years, with the growth of industry and labor and increasing governmental regulation and involvement, such needs have changed dramatically. H.D. Segur has kept pace with such changes. Instead of merely selling insurance, H.D. Segur is involved in the entire field of risk management.

In addition to providing full protection to individuals, the firm serves companies engaged in manufacturing, retailing, wholesaling, service, and real estate development and construction, as well as schools and municipalities. Wherever individuals and companies face a potential exposure from any of their activities, H.D. Segur is prepared to advise cost-effective means of minimizing physical and financial loss.

Segur service goes far beyond ordinary insurance service. In addition to top-notch professionals, the company also has the latest in high technology, with computer programs to determine the most advantageous insurance rates available and the latest data on any claim.

H.D. Segur is one of a handful of independent agencies in the state to offer the services of an in-house loss-control department, with specialists to make periodic surveys of client facilities to evaluate exposures. These highly trained experts can spot many potential hazards and advise on how to correct them before costly losses or accidents occur.

In addition, Segur also specializes in bringing loss-control programs to client facilities. These programs focus on all levels of management—from line supervisors to the chief executive

The services of the H.D. Segur Loss Control Department are available to the firm's commercial accounts.

Personal and commercial account representatives are highly trained to assist clients.

officer—and show how to implement safety programs and motivate workers to observe safety practices. Such programs help train employees in everything from safe driving on the highway to recognizing hidden hazards around machinery in the business.

The firm also provides important help in many other areas of loss prevention, including general liability, product liability, fire safety, security, the elimination of construction hazards, claims management, and timely advice in critical moments.

The firm maintains a strong commitment to minimizing liability exposure through loss control. According to Segur, fewer losses mean lower rates.

At Segur, the client will find a full range of services for individuals and businesses, from personal home and auto, life, and financial services to business coverages including employee benefits and key-man planning. From specially designed shared funding or fully insured programs, to health maintenance organization (HMO) services to pension plans, Segur service is experienced and professional.

Since 1890 H.D. Segur's commitment to service has remained the same, while keeping pace with changing times.

THE CONNECTICUT BANK AND TRUST COMPANY (CBT)

Calvin Coolidge once said, "The business of America is business." Likewise, the business of the greater Waterbury area is The Connecticut Bank and Trust Company.

While part of the $30-billion Bank of New England Corporation, CBT places an emphasis on the local level. Although CBT has more than 160 branches in the state, decisions are localized and made by bankers who know their clients' companies, not by officers in a city miles away with whom they have no rapport.

Each of its regional headquarters, including its Waterbury Community Business Office, is staffed with senior professionals and headed by a regional manager who has full responsibility for banking relationships and significant lending authority. This gives clients the benefit of working within a small bank atmosphere with all the advantages of what is actually one of the state's largest commercial banks.

In Waterbury, CBT provides service in the areas of commercial real estate, community business, and private banking at its Community Business Office at 20 East Main Street. The bank also maintains four branches in the greater Waterbury area.

As Waterbury's renaissance continues, CBT's role in its development is increasingly important. CBT, which was established in 1792, provides interim construction as well as permanent financing on a wide variety of projects for companies in construction as well as for those planning to build a new facility. Real estate loans can be used for land acquisition and development as well as for construction for commercial, industrial, and residential properties.

In the area of community business, CBT takes a consultative approach to lending, working as a team to identify and evaluate lending alternatives and to structure the loan to meet customer needs. It also offers a cash management network that maximizes the productive use of the client's funds and reduces the time a client spends in administering balances.

CBT also provides quality administration of superior investment of pension and profit-sharing plan assets. In addition, its nationally recognized Money Center provides a full range of investment alterna-

The Connecticut Bank and Trust Company has a community business office (shown here) at 20 East Main Street and four branches in the greater Waterbury area, where services are provided in the areas of commercial real estate, community business, and private banking.

tives. CBT also maintains comprehensive and sophisticated international banking services to ensure clients profit from the excellent opportunities offered by foreign trade. With offices strategically located worldwide, more than 400 depository relationships with foreign banks, and one of the nation's top foreign exchange trading operations, CBT simplifies every type of transaction, anywhere in the world.

Private Banking at CBT is for financially successful individuals who require and expect superior service and attention in managing their affairs. CBT's Private Bankers are ready to provide extra dimensions of sophistication, experienced counsel, innovations, and creativity in helping clients make the most of their financial opportunities—to achieve the life-style and security they want for themselves and their families.

The Connecticut Bank and Trust Company's devotion to both individuals and corporations has led to record growth, with the bank tripling its assets in 3.5 years—reaching the $10-billion mark—servicing more and more customers who are ready to demand more from a bank.

BANK OF BOSTON CONNECTICUT

ABOVE: Bank of Boston Connecticut's corporate headquarters is located on the Green, in the heart of downtown Waterbury.

RIGHT: Louis H. Ulizio (right), vice-chairman and Commercial Banking Group executive, and William A. Shea, vice-president and industrial development manager, look over plans on the site of a Waterbury construction project financed by Bank of Boston Connecticut.

The development of a bank and a city go hand in hand. As one grows, so does the other. This has been the underlying philosophy of Bank of Boston Connecticut, formerly Colonial Bank, whose origins date back more than a century.

Modern times demand modern banking methods and responsive banking services. And, in the case of Bank of Boston Connecticut, it means meeting customers' needs through the special Industrial Development Department, which has helped guide Waterbury through some trying times.

Over the past 20 years, because of the migration of the brass industry, Waterbury had begun to fall on hard times. Large mainstay companies, such as Anaconda, Chase Brass, and Scovill, began to close up shop or leave town. Consequently, jobs were lost and unemployment rose. Many storefronts became vacant facades.

At this troubling time Bank of Boston Connecticut (then Colonial) took a leadership position through its Industrial Development Department and made a commit-ment to the city's economic recovery.

And although Waterbury is experiencing a renaissance, the department's position has not changed. Its goal remains to persuade out-of-state firms to locate in Waterbury and to convince firms already there not only to remain, but also to undertake expansion plans in Waterbury.

National statistics show that for every 100 new jobs created in a community, there will be $1.7 million in new payrolls, $1.2 million in new retail sales, one million dollars in new bank deposits, 140 new automobiles registered, and some 65 additional new jobs in sup-port services created.

Such economic growth pumps lifeblood into a city. Through the years Bank of Boston Connecticut, under the guidance of vice-president William Shea, who manages the Industrial Development Department, and vice-chairman Louis Ulizio, has been instrumental in bringing scores of companies to Waterbury and financing their new facilities in industrial parks or the downtown area or other locations. These efforts have created or saved thousands of jobs

and have cycled hundreds of millions of dollars into the city.

Bank of Boston Connecticut, a wholly owned subsidiary of Bank of Boston Corporation, has clearly been a front runner in the city's economic revival. Headquartered in Waterbury at 81 West Main Street, Bank of Boston Connecticut is a full-service commercial bank with 50 branches throughout Connecticut and more than of $2.5 billion in assets. Bank of Boston Connecticut, which has played a prominent role in attracting new business to the area as well as encouraging existing business to remain and expand, maintains a strong commitment to that goal and to the continuing growth of the city.

CIPRIANO & ASSOCIATES

In a classroom in Milan, Italian phrases ripple the air. In a training facility in Spain, the Spanish instructor speaks ardently. In many of these places, they are speaking the same language—the language of Cipriano & Associates.

The Waterbury-based company of human resources consultants offers a wide variety of dynamic training programs that the firm presents itself, as well as offers to corporate trainers and professionals for use in their own training courses.

Don and Mary Ann Cipriano are the backbone of the company, a husband-and-wife team that

Ann Flesor (left) and Cynthia Shahen (right), independent associates, discussing a consultation project with the Ciprianos.

started the firm in their basement and first conducted business meetings at the breakfast table. Through the years they have built their company to the point where it has expanded and moved twice, first to Highland Avenue and then to its present site, in order to better serve its customers. The firm has developed more than three dozen training programs that have been translated into French and Italian.

The Ciprianos and their associates present their programs

throughout the United States as well as abroad. These training programs basically focus on management development and sport such titles as Managing Your Boss, Managing with Style, Maximizing Performance, and the Invisible Motivator. Many *Fortune* 500 companies are on the Cipriano roster of clients. In addition, Cipriano & Associates is the largest distributor for the Minneapolis-based Carlson Learning Company, which produces training materials.

Another aspect of Cipriano & Associates involves the instruction of trainers within large companies, who will, in turn, teach the programs to the company's employees. Such Cipriano-trained instructors give courses to more than 20,000 workers annually.

Cipriano & Associates also provides a needs assessment program for corporations whereby the firm's employees analyze the operations of the company in terms of people skills, communications, and goal clarity. This sophisticated computerized assessment provides a prescription for the firm and, in many cases, needed programs are presented by Cipriano & Associates.

In all of its programs, the Waterbury firm can provide the re-

Don and Mary Ann Cipriano in their office suite.

sources and expertise of the more than 20 associates whose expertise involves all areas of human resource development.

The field is burgeoning, with management development comprising an industry exceeding $32 billion that is projected to grow to $60 billion by 1995, a projection largely based on the information explosion, which mandates the development of both cognitive and interpersonal skills, of which the latter is addressed by Cipriano & Associates.

So when the telephone rings at Cipriano & Associates, just about anyone could be on the other end. The call can come from an executive at a fast-food chain that is developing a program for new managers and wants to review training materials, or it can be from a chief executive officer of a company that has a high turnover rate and low morale, who wants to turn the situation around. Since 1980 Cipriano & Associates has been building its business on high ethics and values, and has provided both troubleshooting prowess and training in the making of better managers.

Photo by Georgia Sheron

Building Greater Waterbury

From concept to completion, Waterbury's building industry and real estate professionals shape tomorrow's skyline.

Drubner Industrials, 212

Connecticut Factors, Inc., 214

Errichetti Associates, 215

Heritage Development Group, Inc., 216

Veeco Inc., 218

United Electrical Contractors, Inc., 220

F.B. Mattson Company Inc., 222

Photo by Georgia Sheron

DRUBNER INDUSTRIALS

As bulldozers scoop up chunks of earth and rock to make way for another new project, Waterbury's progress is clocked, brick by brick, building by building. As old buildings come alive once again and find their place in modern times, Waterbury's renaissance blossoms. More often than not, behind such progress is Drubner Industrials and its president Norman Drubner, the man who has been dubbed "the Donald Trump of Waterbury."

Drubner, an attorney who specializes in real estate law, started the commercial and industrial real estate brokerage firm in 1980. He has logged more than 25 years of experience in the real estate business since he purchased his first building, a 20-unit apartment complex on Willow Street that he still owns today, signing a check for $1,600 with trembling hands.

Drubner Industrials has grown through the years to become a major power in the world of real estate in the greater Waterbury and northwest Connecticut areas, with a variety of projects ranging from renovations to acquisitions to projects built from the ground up. The firm has sought and obtained a position of flexibility, with the capacity to act as either a broker or a principal, either building or purchasing and renovating buildings, then leasing them.

"We wear more than one hat so that we can bring more to the table," says Drubner. "Our ability to act as principal and as broker allows us to perform much better service and provides our customers greater flexibility."

Throughout its history Drubner Industrials, headquartered in the former Anaconda American Brass building on Meadow Street, has become associated with some of the biggest and most elaborate development projects both in Waterbury and in Torrington, where the firm opened its first office outside the Brass City in 1986.

And while the main role of the company is to serve as brokers, it also has undertaken many projects as principal. In 1988, for example, the firm renovated Buckingham Park, at 1100 Buckingham Street in Watertown, formerly the home of the Apparel Fasteners Division of Scovill. Drubner Industrials leased a major portion of the 325,000-square-foot building to Bristol Babcock. In turn, it purchased that company's former executive office building and manufacturing facility at 40 Bristol Street in Waterbury.

One of Drubner's major purchases as principal is 500 Chase Parkway, a 55,300-square-foot building that formerly served as Scovill's

Drubner Industrials is offering luxurious executive offices for lease in the prestigious 500 Chase Parkway building.

world headquarters. Now being offered for lease, it features luxurious executive offices with an emphasis on quality, comfort, and design.

French's Mill, an old tube mill that once had the longest draw of tube in the world, was renovated by Drubner Industrials. The project was completed in 1986, and office space was leased to businesses in the building that had been erected in the early 1900s and added to in the 1920s. Although modernized, it retains the charm of yesteryear.

Another interesting project is the recent development of the 58-acre Kennedy Industrial Park in Torrington. The 11-lot business and industrial complex features an 80,000-square-foot manufacturing plant and a 33,000-square-foot research and development building. The lots there range in size from 2.5 to eight acres.

With the exception of several condominium projects, the majority of Drubner Industrials' efforts is devoted to industrial and commercial development. "Industrial development," according to Drubner, "leads the way. Everything else follows closely. When firms outside the area come here, they bring along a need for housing for their employees and for office and support space."

Drubner predicts a bright future for the Brass City with a strong emphasis as a leading warehouse and distribution center as well as a hub for medium-size light industry, high-tech companies, some light assembly, and research and development firms.

Drubner Industrials works closely with state and city agencies devoted to the economic development of Connecticut in general and Waterbury in particular. "They recognize that this area is on the leading edge, and they really work with brokers. As brokers, we see our role as being a magnet to attract new industry to the area," says Drubner.

Toward accomplishing this goal, Drubner Industrials enjoys a close relationship with its clients by offering financial advice, for example, and by establishing relationships with all lending institutions in the Waterbury, the northwest Connecticut, and even the Hartford areas. The company maintains ex-

Another of the firm's renovations, 414 Meadow Street, is headquarters for Drubner Industrials, a major commercial and industrial real estate brokerage firm in Waterbury and the northwest Connecticut area.

perts on staff to assist in the financial arena and offer hands-on support.

The firm also lends a hand when it comes to the community. In 1988 the Norman S. Drubner Foundation for Charitable Giving was formed with the purpose of providing private financial support to individuals or organizations within Waterbury and some nine surrounding towns. Eligible applicants must be nonprofit and in the educational, cultural, health, religious, or social arenas. The foundation also created a full scholarship program for men and women who reside in the same towns.

Whether it's a charitable contribution or a sizable renovation, Drubner Industrials has made its mark in a community that Norman Drubner says is "vital, healthy, and headed for great things." Drubner Industrials plans to be there every inch of the way.

CONNECTICUT FACTORS, INC.

Gut feelings, foresight, and perseverance are the traits that have propelled Robert V. Matthews, president of Connecticut Factors, Inc., to early success in real estate development. The 31-year-old developer from Waterbury started in 1980 with $2,000 and a dilapidated four-family building. Those two factors have since multiplied into an empire of sorts—in syndications, historic renovations, subdivisions, commercial developments, and Waterbury's first condominium conversions. Today Matthews is a dominant player in the city's ongoing renaissance, with a dozen downtown buildings that he has purchased and renovated, and numerous others that he has built and sold.

"I love old buildings," says Matthews. "Restoring them to what they used to be—that's our niche. If it means digging into the pockets a little deeper to save a stained-glass window, it's still worth it."

Evidence of Matthews' penchant for older buildings can be seen throughout Waterbury. Some of his most noteworthy rehabilitations are his penthouse offices in the historic Bohl's Block Building, the Rectory, and the Frederick buildings on either side of the Palace Theatre, Platt's Corner on East Main Street, the Farrington Building on the Green, and the chamber building, which formerly housed Worth's Smiling Service.

Matthews' energies have also been directed to outside areas; he is involved in several land, marina, and development projects in and around the Waterbury area and in Florida. These and other deals have often been consummated on just a handshake, without a contract.

The snowball effect of these handshake deals has led to Matthews' latest acquisition: Fabricated Metal Products, Inc., a metal-fabricating company in the Waterbury area, with annual sales in excess of $20 million. It is his first

venture into the manufacturing business and a challenge that he enjoys.

When asked if his future lies somewhere beyond this city, Matthews shakes his head, "I started here, and it's where the real meat and potatoes of my success has been. It's where it got bigger. Waterbury has been very good to me."

In turn, Matthews has been good to Waterbury. His board memberships include the Greater Waterbury Chamber of Commerce, the advisory board of Centerbank, the Easter Seals Rehabilitation Center,

the St. Vincent de Paul Society, and the American Indian Archaeological Society.

Beyond his philanthropic activities and keeping both of his companies "lean and mean," Matthews manages to play a bit of polo, fly his airplane, and ride the bridle trails of his Middlebury, Connecticut, estate—and, of course, plan his next project.

Robert V. Matthews, president of Connecticut Factors, Inc., in the atrium of the Farrington Building.

ERRICHETTI ASSOCIATES

The "green" is the centerpiece of a New England city, and at the heart of the Waterbury green is Errichetti Associates, the developer known primarily for most of the rebuilding of the downtown area.

Prominent among such projects is One Exchange Place, an Italian granite-clad office building completed in 1986 that currently houses Errichetti's offices.

The Errichetti name is one that has been well known in Waterbury for more than three decades. Errichetti Associates has developed a variety of significant, nationally recognized residential, retail, and commercial projects. Many of the most dynamic projects in the city bear the Errichetti stamp. These include

Developed by Errichetti Associates and Ocean Properties, Buckingham Square is a mixed-use development of hotel, office, and retail space. The project's centerpiece is a 207-room Holiday Inn Crowne Plaza Hotel. Integrated into the overall design are four historically preserved buildings along Bank Street.

3 Exchange Place, a 10-story office building of stone and blue glass that climbs in steps from an arcade entrance to a loggia below pitched roofs, currently under construction. When constructed, this Waterbury showpiece will mirror with great elegance and natural authority the landmark architecture of the Waterbury Green.

Another prominent project is Buckingham Square, which features the new Holiday Inn Crowne Plaza Hotel, a 207-room hotel, as well as a mixed-use office and retail downtown renewal project. When completed, the center will offer more than 80,000 square feet of office and retail space in addition to the hotel facilities. The project will also incorporate the renovation of four historic buildings.

Other easily recognizable Errichetti projects include Savings Tower, a housing complex for the elderly, and the Abbott Terrace Health Center, a 150-bed long-term health care facility. The firm, in fact, is increasing its concentration in the health care construction field, and will soon be erecting a medical office building on North Elm Street in conjunction with St. Mary's Hospital. This fa-

Three Exchange Place, developed by Errichetti Associates, is a planned 10-story, 100,000-square-foot class A office building located on the City Green in downtown Waterbury. With architectural features that complement the classical buildings surrounding the Green, Three Exchange Place will add a new dimension to the architecture of the city.

cility will contain a diversified range of private medical practices, laboratory and X-ray services, and will provide valet parking, all of which will offer comprehensive care to patients.

A major project on the drawing boards is the construction of the Apple Valley Mall, a 950,000-square-foot regional shopping center expected to be built in the 1990s.

Errichetti has been a significant force in providing quality housing throughout the state with its construction and management of more than 2,500 units.

As the city of Waterbury has grown in both size and stature, Errichetti Associates has been behind much of that growth, providing the city with products designed to fit in with the city's evolution and to stand out with elegance and flair.

HERITAGE DEVELOPMENT GROUP, INC.

It began as the village of the peaceful Pootatuck Indians, who made their home where the gentle hills hugged the Pomperaug River Valley. It was a blessed land, rich with game—a jeweled land sparkling with mirrored ponds, wooded glades, and restful meadows.

Whatever would be built on this site, Henry Paparazzo knew, had to be in complete harmony with nature. When he first conceived the idea of Heritage Village more than two decades ago, Paparazzo instinctively realized that the beauty of the project must be created within nature, not at the expense of it.

This philosophy underscores all of Paparazzo's projects—from the national award-winning 1,000-acre Heritage Village in Southbury, the first such adult condominium in the eastern United States, to a variety of other condominiums, office parks, and other projects scattered

throughout Connecticut, Massachusetts, and New York.

His company, Heritage Development Group, Inc., is an unqualified success. Heritage Village, for example, has been distinguished with numerous awards from the fields of architecture, environmental land planning, and ecology, among them the prestigious First Honor Award of the American Institute of Architects, given in cooperation with *House and Home* and *The American Home* magazines. Heritage Village also has been written about in major magazines such as *Better Homes and Gardens* and *House Beautiful,* and it has been used as a model by many other developers. Heritage Village received the first Award for Excellence in Large Scale Development from the prestigious Urban Land Institute based in Washington, D.C.

Heritage Village is not misnamed. While it depends on the Village of Southbury for essential functions such as police and fire service, it is in many ways self-sustaining, offering such features as its own sewer and water company, a bank, a gas station, and a novelty of retail shops on the premises, as

Henry J. Paparazzo, president of Heritage Development Group, Inc.

well as an extensive recreational facility, including 27 holes of golf. The Harrison Inn conference center and hotel is also located in Heritage Village.

The population of the village is between 4,500 and 5,000 people, residing in 2,700 units. While Heritage Development Group over-

One of the perfect settings that earned Heritage Village in Southbury the coveted Award for Excellence in the Planning, Development, and Use of Land by the prestigious Urban Land Institute.

LEFT: *The Harrison Inn and Conference Center in Heritage Village is Connecticut's only AAA Four-Diamond Resort and Inn.*

BELOW: *The new country club facility at the national award-winning community of Heritage Hills of Westchester.*

sees the functioning of the various retail shops and The Harrison Inn at Heritage Village (residential units are governed by the Master's Association), its attentions are currently devoted to a variety of major projects, such as the development of one of the largest condominium communities in the United States. When Heritage Hills in Westchester County, New York, is completed by the mid-1990s, it will have more than 3,100 condominium units.

Heritage Development Corporation is also planning to develop a four-season resort community in Adams, Massachussets, a public/private effort with the state. It is also planning, in conjunction with Westage Development Group, Inc., of Somers, New York, a number of mixed-use office parks in New York State.

Whether building a condominium community, an office park, or a resort community, the same Heritage philosophy applies—incorporating imaginative land planning, creative architecture, and a deep respect for the environment.

The Heritage Development Group directs its plans and purposes toward the goals of protecting the environment and preserving nature's resources. At Heritage Village, for example, residents can gaze upon wooded views as unspoiled as they were more than two decades ago.

Paparazzo has held this philosophy from his beginning as a developer in the Waterbury area in the 1950s. His dream to expand this concept on a large scale came true with the development of Heritage Village, beginning in the mid-1960s. It was his first major project.

Since that time the Heritage Development Corporation has built more than 8,000 condominium units in the Northeast. "I think our philosophy is that you pay attention to what you are doing, you instill that feeling within your organization, and you develop an organization that is concerned about proper land use, then everyone gets a better project. The people and the community are pleased with the results. We find it worthwhile to put in that extra effort," he says.

A planned community, according to Paparazzo, "is more than a pattern of winding roads, shops, and houses—more than an activities center, swimming pool, and golf course. It is, or can be, a new way of life for the men and women who cross its threshold."

People are the principal concern of The Heritage Development Group. "They are the heart of the Heritage Idea," Paparazzo insists.

And just what is the "Heritage Idea"? It does not lend itself to any easy definition. It is a philosophy—an underlying attitude that inspires Heritage planning, rather than a rigid project formula.

The Heritage Idea combines respect for the land and concern for its people. It brings imagination and courage to community planning. It has vision and purpose. It brings together engineer, architect, banker, historian, and ecologist for the common good. It is concerned with natural beauty, wildlife, clean water, and crisp air.

"Heritage" is defined as something of value handed down from one generation to another. The Heritage Idea looks to the future. Tomorrow's world is being shaped today, and it is the hope of The Heritage Development Group to contribute, in a small but practical way, toward a better world.

VEECO INC.

Design/build is the trend of the future, and Veeco Inc. is there on the forefront. One of the largest electrical, heating, and air conditioning contractors in the area, Veeco's projects include the Glastonbury Corporate Park, in Glastonbury (left); USCG Medical Facility, in Bourne, Massachusetts (below); and the Westview Office Park, in Wallingford (facing page, top).

First a building is just an idea, and then a bunch of lines on paper. The foundation is built and finally, layer by layer, the building is born. For decades to come, maybe even a century or more, the lights of the building will mark the days and nights, and the turning of its thermostat will announce the changing of the seasons.

Veeco Inc., one of the largest electrical, heating, and air conditioning contractors in the area, offers full-service involvement in the entire life-cycle of a structure, from the initial design stage, through the construction, to the maintenance of the building.

Design/build is the trend of the future, and Veeco is there on the forefront. This method, which incorporates input from all subcontractors such as the electrical contractor, provides many benefits to the building owner, including total integration of all systems, more efficient use of time, and lower cost.

"The buzzword in the industry is that it's a 'living building' type of approach," according to Veeco owner Charles Veronneau.

"A building is never permanently stable. In a commercial building, for example, the tenants must arrive and have the heat or the air conditioning on and the building functioning. The building is adaptable to change on an ongoing basis. That's where we come in. Each tenant has different needs."

The company services the commercial, industrial, and institutional markets. Its projects include everything from factories to nursing homes to shopping centers to high rises.

Veeco is growth oriented, a fast-track firm that has grown about 450 percent during the past four years. Much of its progress can be attributed to the design/build approach. Such service-oriented construction ultimately means lower life-cycle cost for the building.

"This requires a lot more flexibility on our part and a lot more planning for the future of the building's life cycle," says Charles Veronneau, the founder and president of the company. "This, we believe, is the way of the future."

The firm also services the retrofit market, as well as upgrading the electrical, heating, and air conditioning systems of existing buildings; energy consumption is of prime concern. Whatever the case Veeco maintains final responsibility for all of its projects.

Company personnel are well versed in the most current equipment, including state-of-the-art ultrahigh-efficiency heating and cooling equipment. They are specially trained in providing the proper heating and air conditioning environments for computer systems and peripheral equipment and do major computer wiring. The firm also supplies and installs power-stabilizing equipment, emergency power generators, and uninterrupted power sources (UPS).

Veeco crews are safety oriented and benefit from periodic training seminars. Employees are dedicated and detail minded, offering an exemplary level of service.

Veeco does not view service

as just a nine-to-five job. The firm provides around-the-clock emergency service and also maintains a large emergency inventory.

Fire evacuation systems are a major focus and and can be provided for most types of buildings, including high rises. The company's largest project to date was the installation of a complete fire alarm system for a major aircraft manufacturer. The project involved 8 miles of conduit, 28 miles of conductor, and the monitoring of some 1,200 sprinkler valves.

Founded in 1983, Veeco offers a management team with more than 30 years of experience and some 25 employees. The business operates out of a modern building on Interstate Lane, centrally located and in close proximity to I-84. Its new location, built in 1986, has some 12,200 square feet of office and inventory space.

The company is optimistic about the future, setting its sights on growth in the areas of computer wiring, power stabilization, emergency and uninterruptible power systems, and in fire evacuation systems. It will continue to offer turnkey electrical services as a prime contractor and to act as a site lighting contractor. In addition, it offers subcontractor coordination, overseeing the work of other contractors. Veeco is also willing to work on venture projects.

Whether the company is "in on the ground floor" or is contracted to maintain a 100-year-old building, Veeco Inc. offers first-class service, constructing and maintaining the electrical, heating, and air conditioning functions of the "living" building.

The electrical power supplied by the main switchgear room is critical to the shops in Watertown's Westwood Plaza. The electrical, heating, and air conditioning systems were designed and installed and are now maintained by Veeco Inc.

UNITED ELECTRICAL CONTRACTORS, INC.

Peter Vaccarelli, owner and general manager.

United Electrical Contractors, Inc., (U.E.C.), started operating in 1971 as a two-man electrical company specializing in service. While Waterbury was evolving from its post-industrial period, the company began a slow growth process that continues to the present. During the 1975 construction recession, the owners returned profits earned by hard work to the growing firm.

Vice-president Peter Vaccarelli explains that he and his brother, Anthony, president of the firm, made a commitment to build a company that housed a strong organization in accordance with a family-business concept. This early commitment brought the firm to its current status as one of Connecticut's leading design/build electrical contractors.

Company expansion was gradual and steady from its first location in Peter's basement in 1971, to a 1,200-square-foot location on Harpers Ferry Road in Waterbury in 1977, and then, in 1982, to Porter Street, where 4,200 square feet held U.E.C. for six years. In April 1988 the firm moved into its new location at Interstate Lane with

4,200 square feet of office space and 10,000 square feet of warehouse space for material and operations managers and inventory control.

The present 35 employees are each individually talented and exemplify the company's ongoing commitment to quality and excellence.

They have also collaborated on the development of in-house technical and management seminars. In addition, U.E.C. has set forth a state-approved apprenticeship program that fosters the development of new trade people.

Currently, about 25 percent of U.E.C.'s business is geared to the residential market, 30 percent to the commercial market, and the remaining 45 percent to the industrial sector. This focus differs from that of the early days, when the overwhelming work concentration was in the residential marketplace. The newest focus for U.E.C. is the design/build market, which the firm initiated in 1984 with a 130,000-square-foot, 175-unit congregate housing project. The design/build concept allows U.E.C. to devise electrical concepts and engineer drawings to an owner's specifications and budget. In this way, a com-

Anthony Vaccarelli, owner and operations manager.

plete electrical construction package can be implemented. An example of this philosophy is the U.E.C. electrical renovation of Armstrong Rubber Company in West Haven, Connecticut, which involved high-voltage distribution, secondary distribution, lighting, and a communications system for a 220,000-square-foot industrial park.

In recent years U.E.C. completed several major electrical projects at Waterbury Hospital, including the hospital's new M.R.I. unit. As the prime contractor for the offices and operating room facilities of a local plastic surgeon, the firm directed the electrical, mechanical, plumbing, and gas system required for the complex.

United Electrical Contractor's most prominent selling feature is superior service at every level, including service calls and design/build installations. "If we can't offer the best service, we really have no advantage over the competition," explains Anthony Vaccarelli. "Response time and quality service are what U.E.C. is all about."

A tightly run organization avail-

able for the needs of the local community and the requirements of the State of Connecticut, United Electrical Contractors, Inc., looks to its highly qualified, loyal employees for the future. As with all successful companies, it is the people who make the difference.

ABOVE: United Electrical Contractors, Inc., moved into its new headquarters in April 1988.

BELOW: On the job with United Electrical Contractors, Inc., whose most prominent selling feature is superior service at every level, including service calls and design/ build installations.

F.B. MATTSON COMPANY, INC.

As workers in hard hats realize architects' visions and the sounds of construction ring through the air, F.B. Mattson Company, Inc., continues to make its mark on the greater Waterbury landscape.

The Mattson Company continues to create quality construction specializing in commercial and institutional building with about 70 percent of its focus being on restoration and renovation work together with many additions to existing facilities.

The Mattson Company is also well known for its high-quality building of architectural mill work and high-quality residential work.

The company was founded in 1947 by Fridolf B. Mattson, a Swedish immigrant who followed in the footsteps of his brothers and whose own efforts in the Waterbury area construction industry date back to the mid-1920s.

Today a third generation of Mattsons guides the company along its path of consistent growth, headed by Roy I. Mattson, Sr., who serves as president and now is assisted by two of his sons, Paul and Peter, who will carry the business into a fourth generation.

The firm, which today employs some 60 workers, focuses on serving a market within a 30-mile radius of Waterbury. Some current projects include the renovation to the west wing of The Bank of Boston Connecticut headquarters; a new office complex for the Naugatuck Savings Bank, Naugatuck, Connecticut; completion of the H.D. Segur Incorporated offices at 255 Bank Street (the same building that houses the Bank of Waterbury); and the interior completion of the law offices of Gager, Henry & Narkis at One Exchange Place.

In addition to construction, the firm also focuses on construction management and is able to supervise all building construction functions.

Through the years Mattson Company has striven to maintain its reputation for excellence and devotion to details, reinforcing its image as a quality-oriented firm. "We are not the average, run-of-the-mill construction company," according to Roy Mattson. "When the call is to have it right, the call comes to us."

Mr. Mattson believes that community involvement is an important segment of business life and has its own rewards and satisfaction in helping to take care of a community that has been kind in return.

Mr. Mattson serves on several boards, including that of American Bank of Connecticut. He also is president of the board of the Woodhall School, a facility that the firm also planned and built.

Quality of Life

Medical and educational institutions contribute to the quality of life of Waterbury area residents.

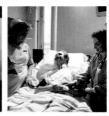

Post College, 226

The Taft School, 228

St. Mary's Hospital, 230

Public Higher Education in Waterbury, 232

Waterbury Hospital Health Center, 234

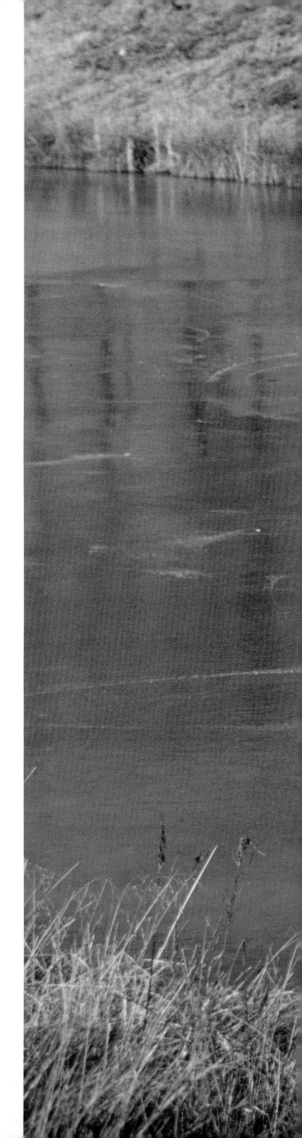

Photo by Georgia Sheron

POST COLLEGE

On the campus of Post College is a camperdown elm tree, unbending through winter gales, sheltering the earth when the summer sun beats down. That strong, sturdy elm is the college's symbol, depicting academic excellence that is rooted deep in quality.

It is a tradition preserved since the college's founding in 1890 as a private business school. Since then Post College has undergone many academic and physical changes in response to the community's need for expanded educational services, moving from downtown Waterbury to its present 70-acre campus on Country Club Road in 1965. Ten years later it made the transition from a junior college to an accredited, four-year college offering both bachelor and associate degree programs, and it expanded to serve a residential as well as a commuting student body.

And while Post College has continually progressed, its continuing success is based, as it has been since the beginning, on bringing out students' individual abilities and developing their knowledge and confidence to carry them forward. The college motto, *Te Cognosce* (Know Thyself), symbolizes a personalized approach to each student.

Post College has undergone many academic and physical changes since its founding in 1890 as a private business school. Today it is located on a 70-acre campus and is a four-year college, offering both bachelor and associate degree programs.

This is accomplished in an environment that inspires academic excellence. The college fosters a warm, friendly environment, one in which communication is encouraged between students and staff. A diversity of academic programs, small classes, and a close relationship among students, faculty, and administration characterize the college.

An independent, nonprofit, coeducational institution, the school's enrollment of more than 1,700 full- and part-time students represents a wide range of academic, social, economic, and cultural backgrounds, providing a stimulating opportunity for students to gain new insights and perspectives through their college association.

Post offers a Bachelor of Science degree in Business Administration in accounting, management, and marketing and Bachelor of Arts degrees in English, history, psychology, and sociology. In addition, there are many associate-level degrees in a large number of areas, in-

cluding early childhood education, equine studies, therapeutic recreation, fashion design, general studies, and business administration.

The picturesque campus includes an academic building complex, a library and Learning Resources Center, a Student Center, a residence complex of five halls, the Drubner Conference Center, and an administration building. It is a secure, peaceful campus, affording students the opportunity to study and learn in an environment free of the hustle and bustle so typified by large universities.

But if students cannot come to the college, Post has seven off-campus sites, including a center at the Danbury Federal Correctional Institute, where evening programs are offered to prisoners.

The college, which has matriculation agreements with Mattatuck Community College, the University of New Haven Graduate School, and the University of Hartford Business School, received a rare 10-year accreditation cycle status in 1988.

Post is devoted to the community, offering a variety of cultural programs such as a summer music series and lectures by such speakers as Hank Aaron, Shirley Chisolm, and William Proxmire.

POST COLLEGE MANAGEMENT CENTER

Where do you go to become a better manager? How do you learn to hire or to fire? What are the latest laws and their implications regarding unemployment compensation?

With hundreds of such questions facing managers in today's complex world, the Post College Management Center is a panacea for business problems, providing not only answers but insights.

Devoted to serving the area's business and industry population, the center provides a variety of practical, hard-hitting courses on subjects that most concern managers,

executives, and business owners. Clearly filling a niche and a need, the Center's accomplishments are manifested in its incredible growth, some 60 percent in 1986 alone. The Center offers more than 100 different courses, ranging from credit management to performance appraisals at its conference Center on Country Club Road and at seven satellite locations. It also offers in-house programs for various companies.

Courses are either noncredit or offer Continuing Education credits. In addition, the Center offers a Certificate in Human Resource Management. The Center also runs a relicensing certificate program for real estate brokers and appraisers, who must take 12 hours of education in state-approved courses each year. The Center serves some 3,500 such students annually.

In addition to courses offered at Post College and other sites, including work places, the Management Center offers a number of special institutes. The Tax Institute helps keep professional people, including lawyers and accountants,

The Post College Management Center offers more than 100 different courses on subjects that most concern managers, executives, and business owners at its conference center and seven satellite locations.

abreast of changes in the tax laws. The Center's Financial Planning Institute helps people interested in exploring financial options, including such topics as valuing a closely held business.

The Post College Management Center also offers an Entrepreneurial Institute to encourage and enhance the spirit of entrepreneurship, as well as to create such a spirit in employees of businesses and organizations interested in starting their own businesses.

A Real Estate Investment Institute offers the latest information on real estate laws and opportunities. Finally, the Center offers a special Institute for Women in Business, where professional female workers can explore common interests, and gain support and receive advice about career advancement.

The Management Center also has a full-scale program to train people in various disciplines in the effective use of computers, ranging from word processing to more complex areas of programming. The goal of the facility is to become a full-service training Center for computer software.

The Post College Management Center also hosts a variety of conferences, including the Women in Business annual seminar, co-sponsored with the U.S. Small Business Administration. The Center also hosts an Employee Assistance Conference, a Credit Management Conference, and a Conference in Entrepreneurship.

With a variety of such offerings, the Post College Management Center provides a unique opportunity for the business and industrial community, based on the belief that education and growth go hand in hand. The goal of the Center is to offer education to improve profitability and productivity, providing for a healthier climate for the business community.

THE TAFT SCHOOL

Behind the picturesque Gothic facades of the buildings on The Taft School's 200-acre campus in nearby Watertown, learning is accomplished in more ways than just "by the book."

Taft, a private boarding school with 400 boarding and 100 day students, tries not only to instill academic knowledge but also to provide an integrated educational experience that will challenge students to give their best in both their intellectual and personal lives.

At Taft, students gather from across the nation and from more than 20 foreign countries, lured by a reputation that dates back some 100 years to 1890, when the school was founded by Horace Dutton Taft, brother of William Howard Taft, the 27th president of the United States. The school's founder stressed the wholeness of the individual—the essential interdependency of growth in both the academic and personal realms.

It is a thriving, living philosophy put into action each day by a stimulating daily schedule that involves classes, lectures or seminar meetings, job duty, exercise, and a special period called Vespers, at which time the headmaster, school chaplain, or others from the Taft community often speak on current issues and ethical themes.

Daily activities are many and varied with a large variety of clubs, sports, and other undertakings. For example, students might spend their spare time in the computer laboratory, the woodworking shop, the darkroom, or backstage in the school's theater. You might find them reading in the library, building models, working on arts projects, talking with teachers, or taking a walk in the country.

Or you might find them volunteering in the community. Taft maintains an active volunteer services program. Nearly one-third of the students work on a one-to-one basis in inner-city schools in Waterbury, with retarded children at Southbury Training School, as teachers'

Taft's reputation for scholastic excellence and challenging variety of activities attracts students from across the nation and more than 20 foreign countries.

helpers in the Watertown Public Schools, and at hospitals, convalescent homes, and day-care centers.

Taft students are known for their concern and their accomplishments. Taft is an active, vital place, and its energies are immediately apparent to even the most casual vis-

The Taft School, a private boarding school in nearby Watertown, dates back to 1890. Founder Horace Dutton Taft was the brother of the 27th president of the United States, William Howard Taft.

Taft offers a rigorous academic program with a broad range of courses from Mandarin Chinese to Physics.

itor. Taft students are not passive pedestrians—they are active doers.

Some basic goals set forth by current headmaster Lance Odden, only the fourth headmaster since the school was founded, include:

—Developing the ability to assimilate and assess the knowledge of man, to think logically, and to communicate thoughts persuasively both on paper and in speech.

—Developing the creative and imaginative impulses that are uniquely one's own through various creative activities.

—Developing new sources of personal strength and confidence through testing oneself in physical adventure.

—Developing one's ability to live with, to work with, to share with, and to serve and lead others in the school community.

—Developing one's ability to choose, to make value judgments about intellectual, extracurricular, and personal life, and in so doing to learn to discriminate between the ephemeral and that which is of lasting value.

Toward these goals, the school offers a rigorous academic program with a broad range of courses from Mandarin Chinese to Physics. In addition, students excel in both sports and art programs.

The athletic program is sufficiently broad and varied to encourage both the physical and psychological growth of students, with each student's athletic experience designed to provide him or her with a chance to engage in a satisfying athletic challenge. The program aims to play a significant role in the development of the student as a person.

The school also offers many opportunities that lie beyond the reach of academics and athletics. Development in the arts is essential to the imaginative, emotional, and aesthetic growth of all students. The arts at Taft embrace the musical arts, the theater arts, dance, and the visual arts.

Taft has gained much recognition for its theater program, which features two professionally equipped theaters and offers opportunities for up to 200 students per year to appear in one of its nine main-stage or laboratory theater productions. For more serious-minded actors, the Taft Repertory Company provides the opportunity to experience conservatory training in a fruitful blend of performance and

academic study. Each year this group of actors and actresses tours schools throughout New England, and has even performed before audiences in Canada, England, Greece, and France, winning scores of awards for acting and production.

In addition to the regular academic year, The Taft School offers two summer programs. The first is a summer school program, which is preparatory rather than remedial in nature and attracts students from as far away as Russia, France, and Spain. Another special summer program is the Taft Educational Center for Teachers, which draws teachers from throughout the Northeast and elsewhere, and offers seminars on a number of subjects, such as teaching advanced placement, language, science, and humanities courses. The program is offered for six weeks in weekly sessions, with more than 600 teachers participating each summer.

The most important growth The Taft School emphasizes is the growth of its students as well-rounded individuals who will one day make significant contributions to society.

Taft's athletic program encourages physical and psychological growth through an individually designed program.

ST. MARY'S HOSPITAL

A man suffering from atherosclerosis of the leg receives advanced cardiovascular therapy with the help of laser devices. A doctor, sitting in his office in a Waterbury suburb, punches in his access code on a computer and knows his patient's lab test results while she is still in the laboratory. A physician looks at a young woman's heart chambers, valves, and coronary arteries through a small radiographically guided heart catheter.

That's the high-tech world of St. Mary's Hospital.

It's Christmastime, and nurse Pat Dwyer's office resembles San-

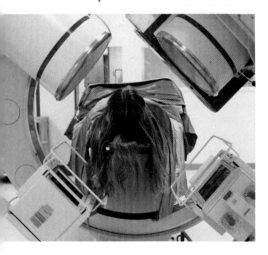

St. Mary's has the latest medical technology available. Photo by Robert A. Lisak

ta's toyshop with piles of colorfully wrapped gifts collected from hospital employees to be given to children at St. Mary's Pediatric Ambulatory Care Center.

It's 9 p.m. and a nurse on the floor notices a patient is still awake. She stands beside his bed with her hand resting gently on his shoulder and comforts him with encouraging words about his progress. Reassured, he smiles in response and closes his eyes to sleep.

That's the high-touch world of St. Mary's Hospital.

While the hospital has changed greatly since it first opened in 1909, it has preserved the tradition of caring and provid-

ing individualized service while remaining in the forefront of a rapidly changing technological age.

Space-age technology is a fact of life at St. Mary's. The hospital, for example, houses its Magnetic Resonance Imaging department in a tempered steel room. The MRI employs a large magnet, radio waves, and a computer to create seemingly miraculous images of internal anatomy, allowing radiologists and surgeons to make diagnoses without surgery.

The hospital is also on the leading edge of laser surgery with the only Vascular Argon Laser in Northeast Connecticut. St. Mary's also

As a teaching hospital St. Mary's physicians and staff are actually involved in clinical research and the enhancement of patient care. Photo by Robert A. Lisak

Conveniently located off Exit 22 of I-84, St. Mary's offers easy access to 13 surrounding towns. Photo by Robert A. Lisak

offers other comprehensive laser surgical procedures including vascular; ear, nose, and throat; gynecological; and orthopedic. Lasers are also used in general surgery for such purposes as liver and tissue resections and the removal of hemorrhoids, minimizing tissue damage, allowing for more precision, and lessening pain.

Cardiac care at St. Mary's Hospital involves some of the most comprehensive and sophisticated systems available, including the first mobile coronary care unit in New England and the multifactorial rehabilitation program, both of which have won awards from the New England Hospital Assembly. St. Mary's

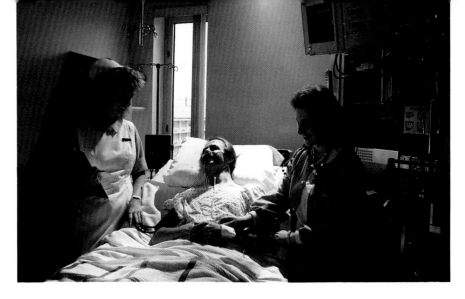

The hospital is widely known for a caring approach to high-tech medicine. Photo by Robert A. Lisak

has a 26-bed coronary care unit, one of the largest and most modern in the state, as well as a state-of-the-art cardiac catheterization lab. Cardiologists rely on the on-sight testing facilities such as nuclear scanning, exercise stress testing devices, and echocardiography (including doppler and 24-hour color-flow monitoring).

A hospital is much more than the technology within it. St. Mary's Mission is a living commitment of caring, one that includes education. With an emphasis on wellness, St. Mary's Hospital has proven its ability to adapt to the changing needs of the community.

The hospital's Center for Health Promotion served more than 10,000 people in its first four years of operation, people who have turned to the center to quit smoking, lose weight, learn about natural childbirth, manage stress, and become more informed on current health issues through more than 40 class offerings. The center provides many of these programs and other health services to area businesses and industries.

Similar courses are also available at St. Mary's Walk-In and Wellness Center at 600 Rubber Avenue in Naugatuck, which also offers health education, a walk-in medical service for minor medical problems, laboratory and radiology services, mental health counseling, and health screening. The Walk-In and Wellness Center also hosts a free community health information series, supplying information about certain health-related conditions, including the "I Can Cope" series for cancer support.

Another satellite location is the Suburban Medical Center in Cheshire, a multispecialty practice that

also offers wellness programs. The Naugatuck Valley Surgical Center at the Old French's Mill on Robbins Street offers comprehensive facilities for uncomplicated elective procedures not requiring a hospital or overnight stay, thus serving patients more efficiently and economically.

St. Mary's maintains several centers at the hospital for specialty areas. The Women's Center for Breast Health provides information regarding breast health and breast disease and guidance in making breast self-examination and mammography part of a regular health routine. The latest low-dose mammography is used to achieve the earliest detection of breast cancer possible.

The Joseph Center is also located at the hospital, offering the first ambulatory alcoholism detoxification unit based in a general hospital in Connecticut. It also offers the Evening Treatment Program, which was the first nonresidential intensive alcoholism treatment program when it opened in 1977 and

has served as a model for many similar programs. In addition, the center provides a continuing-care program, a family counseling unit, and a consultation/liaison service. The hospital's Marian Center, another component of St. Mary's Hospital Psychiatric Services, offers a variety of mental health services, including an inpatient program, ambulatory care, and a partial-hospitalization program.

"Caring" at St. Mary's extends to the employees as well as the people they serve. With nearly 2,000 dedicated employees, the hospital recognizes the need to assist them with as many resources as possible, including education, child care, and other sources. The new Child Development Center offers a full-day program planned to meet the social, language, cognitive, emotional, and physical needs of employees' children. The hospital also offers an Employees Assistance Program, a counseling and referral service for employees and their families. At St. Mary's Hospital, the health caring center, the delivery of health care is based on a tradition of caring and a standard of excellence. Because of this duality of purpose, there is a comfortable mix of high tech and high touch.

Nurses at St. Mary's enjoy a variety of career options and opportunities. Photo by Robert A. Lisak

PUBLIC HIGHER EDUCATION IN WATERBURY

The Higher Education Center offers a variety of educational opportunities to area residents. Photo by Ed Nolan

A mother who has spent the past 15 years raising her children, a high school student with big dreams but a not-so-big budget who wants a quality education or an industrial worker who wants to upgrade his skills in this rapidly changing world of technology can go to the Central Naugatuck Valley Region Higher Education Center and to The University of Connecticut's Hillside campus.

A unique concept in education, the Higher Education Center is home to Mattatuck Community College, The University of Connecticut at Waterbury, and Waterbury State Technical College. It offers a smorgasbord of educational opportunities for area residents, augmented by a Student Center, Learning Resources Center, a Fine Arts Center, and other shared facilities.

MATTATUCK COMMUNITY CENTER

As the students wait by the elevators, they talk animatedly, flipping through books. In the classrooms, instructors enthusiastically impart knowledge. There is a certain magic that happens every day at Mattatuck Community College.

The magic is learning and is available to all. Mattatuck Community College offers students a chance for a quality college education, whether it is the first two years of a four-year degree, a two-year career program, or remediation that prepares students to begin college-level studies.

Mattatuck, created by the Connecticut State Legislature in 1967, offers intellectual challenges to its 4,000 students with some 28 degree and 18 certificate programs in fast-growing fields, including food service, nursing, allied health, auto technology, and computer science. Outside the classroom students can enhance their academic lives with a variety of activities in the arts, music, drama, science, and computers. They can even stargaze through the center's 14-inch Celestron telescope.

The Continuing Education Division offers diverse noncredit learning in areas that range from fine arts to business management. Noncredit courses attract people of all ages including high achieving elementary and middle-school students participating in the summer Kids on Campus program.

Mattatuck Community College extends its learning into the community. The college offers businesses on-site classes that are especially de-

signed for the company. One example is the college's Mobile Training Unit, a computer-equipped classroom on wheels. Project Reach offers adults in the community a series of courses to help in deciding whether returning to school is for them.

Whether on campus or out in the greater Waterbury area, Mattatuck Community College lives its middle name by fostering a sense of community, providing educational opportunities in a warm, caring atmosphere.

THE UNIVERSITY OF CONNECTICUT AT WATERBURY

The Benedict-Miller House with its ornate trimmings and wide porch, its bold contrasts of color, texture, and materials, is the centerpiece of the Hillside Campus of The University of Connecticut at Waterbury.

The lofty Victorian edifice is symbolic of the university's grand heritage and tradition. But UCONN at Waterbury has a modern side, too, as a university that is working hard to meet the needs of the future by providing academic offerings at both its Hillside Campus and its facilities at the Higher Educa-

Nursing is one of 28 degree and 18 certificate programs available at Mattatuck Community College. Photo by Ed Nolan

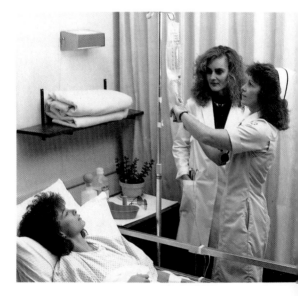

tion Center.

Providing curricular and performance standards that are identical throughout the entire University of Connecticut system, the Waterbury regional campus offers a comprehensive freshman-sophomore curriculum as well as upper-division and graduate courses. The university has extension courses, certificate programs, summer sessions, nondegree enrollment, and a continuing education office. It offers senior citizens the opportunity to audit courses for a nominal fee per semester.

UCONN at Waterbury even offers a Bachelor of General Studies program, a degree awarded to individuals who successfully complete an individualized, interdisciplinary program of part-time study.

The Waterbury branch, created in 1946 after an extension program had been established some four years earlier, serves 800 full-time students each year, with programs offered through the Colleges of Liberal Arts & Science and Agricultural and Natural Resources, as well as through the Schools of Family Studies, Engineering, Education, Business Administration, Allied Health Professions, Pharmacy, and Nursing. Its Cooperative Education Program integrates classroom learn-

The Benedict Miller House on The University of Connecticut's Hillside campus.

ing and work experience.

The city's only university, UCONN's goal is to provide a university education of highest quality while maintaining a climate conducive to the maximum creation, preservation, and transmission of knowledge.

WATERBURY STATE TECHNICAL COLLEGE

In an over-size classroom, the factory of the future with computerized machinery, robots, conveyors, and camera monitors features shows students the door to tomorrow. Waterbury State Technical College holds the key to the future of the area's industry, training today's students for tomorrow's jobs in the technologies.

WSTC offers associate degree programs in automated manufacturing engineering technology, chemical engineering technology, computer-aided drafting/design technology, data-processing technology, electrical engineering technology, general engineering technology, mechanical engineering technology, quality-assurance technology, industrial management technology, environmental management technology,

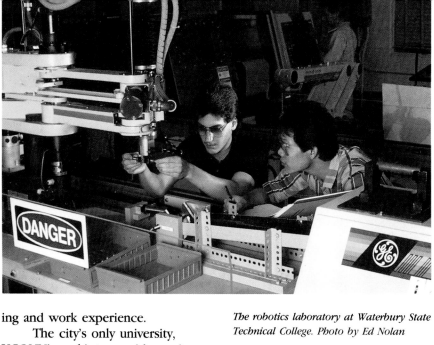

The robotics laboratory at Waterbury State Technical College. Photo by Ed Nolan

fire technology and administration, and optical technology. It also offers certificate programs in quality control, industrial drafting, plastics, and industrial environmental hazardous waste management. A special program is being developed to apply computer-aided drafting/design techniques to the field of horticulture.

The mission of the college is to train students in order to maintain the area's competitive edge in industry. Leading-edge areas are targeted and a curriculum offered to provide Waterbury with the best and the brightest in the world of technology.

The school also provides services to the business community via specially designed classes and programs geared to help workers upgrade their skills. Classes are often held at the company's location, either on a credit or noncredit basis.

WSTC also has a commitment to providing education for minorities, working with local high schools for a special four-session tuition-free program called Computers & You that offers computer basics to minority students. The SITE (Students In Technical Education) 10-week program offers minorities information in computer literacy, science and mathematics careers, the school's mentoring program, as well as general opportunities at the college. The college also offers a new High Tech program for 70 students during the summer. The three-hour-per-day program offers information in the areas of electronics, robotics, CAD, and science.

WATERBURY HOSPITAL HEALTH CENTER

On January 19, 1890, the ladies of Waterbury put on their best bonnets and bustle skirts and the gentlemen got out their best top hats and frock coats for Hospital Sunday. They had been working and waiting seven years for this day—ever since a charter was granted for a hospital.

When the collection plates were passed in Waterbury's churches that day, $1,016.90 was collected for the hospital—in addition to all that the townspeople had donated during the past seven years. After the services the citizens of Waterbury were invited to tour the brand-new facility—one of the most modern in the state.

Entering from a spacious hallway, they found the matron's quarters, a parlor, a reserve ward, a kitchen, a bathroom, and a conservatory on the first floor. Patient wards occupied the second and third floors. Eight physicians and six nurses staffed the 30-bed hospital.

A trauma patient is received via a Life Star helicopter at the new heliport at Waterbury Hospital.

Waterbury at dawn.

Today more than 350 physicians and almost 700 nurses care for up to 14,000 inpatients each year in Waterbury Hospital Health Center's 505-bed facility. Each year 37,000 people visit the emergency room, and 10,000 patients undergo inpatient surgery. As a teaching hospital affiliated with the medical schools of Yale University and the University of Connecticut, Waterbury offers a variety of residencies to new doctors who are pursuing advanced training in specialty areas.

The hospital also participates in programs with other area schools for the education of registered and licensed practical nurses and other health care professionals.

The hospital continues to evolve with the support of the community and now offers a full range of services to support its citizens—from the moment they are born, and before.

For moms-to-be and new mothers, Waterbury Hospital offers Motherwell™, a highly specialized maternity health and fitness program. The eight-session course provides a nonstrenuous, professionally designed, enjoyable exercise system to help pregnant women be more comfortable and stay more active during pregnancy and more easily resume normal activities after delivery.

Waterbury Hospital will soon institute one of the newest approaches to childbirth—the Single

A surgeon escorts a child soon to undergo surgery at Waterbury Hospital's One-Day Surgery Center.

Room Maternity (SRM) concept. Instead of being moved from a labor room to a delivery room to a recovery room to a hospital room as birth progresses, a woman can proceed peacefully through all phases of labor, delivery, recovery, and postpartum in the same modern, pleasantly decorated room. The emphasis is on comfort for mom, dad, and the entire family.

For expectant brothers and sisters, the hospital offers sibling classes. Part of the family-centered maternity program, the class provides siblings and parents with information that will help children adjust to the arrival of the new baby. The session also helps prepare the child for separation from the mother during her hospital stay.

For children who are patients, the hospital's pediatric unit provides quality care in a nurturing setting, recognizing the special fears and concerns of little ones. For instance, a special booklet explains in children's terms that an electroencephalogram—a non-invasive method of measuring brain waves—is nothing more than "your head talking."

To better serve patients of all ages, the hospital has recently added a helipad to accept trauma patients and to transport patients by

Non-invasive cardiac procedures are conducted in the new Cardiac Catheterization Lab.

helicopter.

The One-Day Surgery Center at Waterbury Hospital makes it possible for many patients to undergo their procedure before noon and be home in time for dinner. This is particularly good news for children, who often fear being away from home more than the procedure itself.

Waterbury Hospital offers magnetic resonance imaging (MRI)—the newest and most sophisticated system for visualizing the body's internal organs and tissues. Using a radio frequency signal and the power of a magnet 30,000 times stronger than the earth's magnetic field, the MRI painlessly generates an image of the brain, nerves, tendons, ligaments, and blood vessels to help physicians diagnose neurological disease, vascular and heart disease, and orthopedic conditions.

The hospital's Cardiac Catheterization Laboratory provides a non-invasive method of diagnosing and opening blocked arteries that can often eliminate the need for open-heart surgery.

The Cardiac Rehabilitation Program is designed to help those

Hospital employees enjoy a brisk workout at the new employee fitness center.

who have undergone heart attacks or cardiac surgery to return to a normal and healthier life-style, with monitored exercise and dietary consultation.

The hospital offers a broad spectrum of psychiatric services, including a 40-bed inpatient service—the largest of all general hospitals in Connecticut, outpatient services, emergency room services, psychiatric liaison and consultation services, and community education programs. The hospital's psychiatric care is augmented by an affiliation with the Institute of Living in Hartford, which provides educational exchanges and in-service training for professional staff and students, as well as a referral base and aftercare services for patients and their families.

While the hospital is on the leading edge of medicine and technology, it also takes a personal approach, offering caring of the highest quality from the top down and the bottom up. With this commitment comes a host of special programs, including several for senior citizens. Meals for Seniors offers nutritious, low-cost dinners to those 60 and older in the hospital's cafeteria daily at 4 p.m.—with free parking in the hospital's parking lots.

A Senior Health Awareness Center offers blood pressure screenings, blood sugar screenings, cholesterol screenings, a Better Breathing Club, an Alzheimer's support group, and sessions on a wide range of topics including nutrition, diabetes, poison prevention, and cancer control.

The Woman's Program at the Waterbury Hospital Health Center offers support and educational programs for women entering menopause, battered women, mastec-

tomy patients, and candidates for cesarean birth. The program also offers a New Parent Survival Camp, Lamaze classes, and many other courses and classes for women of all ages.

As part of its commitment to reach out to the community, the hospital has established a satellite service in Southbury, and will soon add services in Naugatuck and Thomaston. These facilities provide quality health care to residents of those communities who find it difficult to travel a distance to receive medical treatment.

The hospital, which is the city's largest employer with between 1,500 and 2,000 employees, makes every effort to retain its high-quality staff by providing benefits such as an on-site day-care center, a physical fitness center, tuition reimbursement, educational programs, and annual events such as picnics and Employee Recognition Day. This commitment to its em-

ployees is part of Waterbury Hospital Health Center's broader concern: offering the best patient care to the community.

Waterbury Hospital's reputation has spread as far as the Soviet Union. In 1988 a team of Soviet physicians came to the hospital to study orthopedic methods in an exchange program between the United States and the Soviet Union.

From the very beginning, on Hospital Sunday, the citizens of Waterbury have supported their hospital. More than 375 men, women, and young people continue to offer the gift of their time and skills as volunteers.

As the city of Waterbury grows, Waterbury Hospital evolves to meet new needs. With the opening in 1972 of the 11-floor, $18.8-million Pomeroy Pavilion, Waterbury Hospital Health Center became one of the largest and most modern medical facilities in Connecticut. State-of-the-art equipment and facilities, combined with a trained and dedicated staff, assures the highest caliber of health care and support for the community as the hospital enters its second century of commitment and caring.

The Greater Waterbury Imaging Center houses the new Magnetic Resonance Imager (MRI) at Waterbury Hospital.

The Marketplace

Waterbury's retail establishments, service industries, and products are enjoyed by residents and visitors to the area.

Torrington Supply Co., Inc., 240

J.E. Smith & Co., 242

Checkmark Office Supply, Inc., 243

The Starbuck Sprague Company, 244

Courtesy, Waterbury Convention and Visitors Commission

TORRINGTON SUPPLY CO., INC.

For a long time the building was just a dream. Then it came a step closer to reality in the guise of a blueprint, which hung on the wall in Harold Stein's office, in a building that had been erected when Abraham Lincoln was president.

In 1988 the dream came true—all 70,000 square feet of it, the combination warehouse, showroom, and offices of Torrington Supply Co., Inc., a plumbing, heating, and industrial supply house founded in 1917 by Harold's father, David Stein.

In 1987 the firm was ranked as the 82nd-largest plumbing supply house in the country. But back

The dream of a new building became a reality in December 1988, when Torrington Supply Co., Inc., moved into its 73,000-square-foot warehouse, showroom, and offices.

then the operation, although quality and service oriented, was somewhat piecemeal because the company was forced to work out of five separate warehouses.

Today all that has changed. The new building isn't only a showroom, it's a showplace. "We have the most beautiful showroom between New York and Boston," says Stein, who serves as the company's president.

A number of model bathrooms are set up in the showroom, including 10 that are fully operational and feature state-of-the-art design and such amenities as whirlpools, saunas, and automatic toilets

and lavatories. The firm does not sell in the retail market; however, plumbing contractors, designers, and architects are invited to bring in their clients to view and make selections from the showroom.

The showroom isn't the only part worth showing off. The warehouse, designed by Footlick Associates of Chicago, a leading warehouse designer, incorporates the latest in warehousing design, which allows for maximum efficiency. While all handling of goods in the old warehouses was done by hand, the new facility has a conveyor on all three levels of shelving and four electric material stackers.

The office is laid out for maximum use of the latest computer technology.

The firm, one of the largest in southern New England, caters to four basic markets: plumbing and heating contractors; industrial customers; water, gas, and electric utilities; and institutions such as hospitals and government facilities.

The company's strength is distributing the best quality items and training its personnel so they have good product knowledge and can thus provide outstanding service. There is a continuing training program for all personnel as well as several training sessions per year for customers to familiarize them with specialized or new products.

The firm's staffing ensures that each and every customer, large or small, will receive individualized service. Accompanying the new building are new service-oriented features, such as an industrial specialties department, which offers specialized technical assistance as well as in-plant repair of compressors, pumps, turbines, automated valves, and heat exchangers.

Another innovation is the addi-

tion of a sophisticated Siemen's Saturn phone system that allows customers to enter orders on a 24-hour-a-day, seven-day-a-week basis. In addition, the building features a 42-foot-long customer service counter.

The company has always prided itself on the service orientation that provides around-the-clock emergency service. If, for example, a hospital should experience a water-main break at 3 a.m., its plant engineer would call a special number and be met at Torrington Supply by an on-call expert who would be able to furnish the needed parts.

Keys to the success of Torrington Supply Co., Inc., have been the loyalty and repeat business of its customers, who know they'll have access to an extensive inventory that includes plumbing fixtures, pumps, heating boilers, radiators, pipe, valves and fittings, temperature and pressure indicators, regulators, and the largest and most diversified stock of water heaters, unit heaters, and ball valves in Connecticut. The company also has an area in its new shop that is devoted to the repair of industrial pumps, and trained professionals assemble and test automated Jamesbury ball

Officers of the company include (seated, from left) Morris Stein, chairman of the board; Harold Stein, president; and (standing, from left) Joel Becker, vice-president and treasurer; Nancy Becker, secretary; and Fred Stein, vice-president.

valves.

The firm maintains a fleet of 12 trucks and seven outside sales persons to serve customers. In addition to its two major product lines, American Standard and A.O. Smith, Torrington Supply features a wide variety of products from other manufacturers, including Goulds Pumps, Dresser, H.B. Smith, Burnham, Mueller, Nibco, Jamesbury, Tranter, Trane, Cuno, Aquaglass, Elkay, Grin-

nell, and many others.

The company was founded in 1917 as Brass City Plumbing Supply, but the name was changed in 1934 to Torrington Supply Co., Inc., when the firm was incorporated.

It remains a family business. Morris Stein serves as chairman of the board, and a second brother Jerome recently retired as president. Now there is a third generation involved in the company: Fred Stein, son of Morris, is vice-president, and his brother-in-law, Joel Becker, is vice president/operations. Fred's sister, Nancy Becker, has recently joined the firm.

The family atmosphere pervades the business, which boasts of many long-term employees, including six with more than 40 years' experience with the company. Through the years the "family" has extended outward into the community, with principals and employees offering much in the way of community service. Morris Stein, for example, is a past president of Waterbury Hospital as well as the New England and national trade associations.

The key to Torrington Supply Co., Inc., says Stein, is its people. "Without good people, we're just another supply house. People are our most dependable—and valuable—asset."

Service is provided by knowledgeable personnel, and an extensive inventory assures repeat business from satisfied customers.

J.E. SMITH & CO.

In 1897, when J.E. Smith & Co. was founded by James Emile Smith, formerly a bookkeeper with a Waterbury lumber company, the population of the city was roughly 45,000. As the city grew building by building, it was often with the help of J.E. Smith lumber, building supplies, and hardware products.

In its almost a century of operation, J.E Smith & Co. has grown from a small firm specializing in lumber, mill work, and roofing, to a large company offering a broad range of building products for the commercial and retail market.

As Waterbury expanded, so did J.E. Smith—a family-run firm now in its third generation—providing the products needed by builders and home owners alike. After J.E. Smith died in 1912, the firm was taken over by his son, J. Francis Smith, who was president until his death in 1959. Subsequently, the company was overseen by his brother, Edmund, who retired in 1982, and his brother, Steele, who served as vice-president. John "Jack" Smith is the firm's current president.

J.E. Smith has proven itself to be a company of stamina, surviving two fires and a flood. In 1936 a blaze destroyed a yard in the west end of town. On August 19, 1955, a day labeled Connecticut's Black Friday, the ravaging waters of the Naugatuck Valley did not spare J.E. Smith; much of the building was under water.

Rallying, the company soon reopened, only to be hit again with disaster two years later, when a general alarm fire—the city's first in 12 years—destroyed building materials, company vehicles, and neighboring buildings. Again the firm showed its resiliency. Sales volume for the month after the fire even topped that of the same month of the previous annum.

By the following year new buildings were erected on Bank Street to replace the operation's former home on Benedict Street. In

Advice from experienced salespeople and the latest in quality products is assured when shopping at J.E. Smith & Co. for hardware, lumber, and building material.

1986 the entire facility was renovated, inside and out, and the retail shop expanded from 10,000 to 14,000 square feet.

While there have been many changes for the company over the years, J.E. Smith's commitment to service and quality products has remained intact. The firm maintains a retail shop where well-versed employees wait on customers, offering advice on products and building methods. There is always a bustle of activity around the sales counter, where customers, including everyone from do-it-yourselfers to professional builders, ask questions ranging from "Is the foam insulation in the can flame retardant?" to "What is the horsepower on this grainer?"

The company also has a con-tract hardware department to better service commercial hardware customers, and a growing wholesale and mail-order division.

While the retail shop accounts for approximately 15 percent of the firm's sales, the overwhelming majority of the company's business is lumber products. Still, newcomers to the store are often amazed by the wide variety of products as well as by the staff's knowledge about each individual item.

Some things have changed. There is no longer, as a 1915 bill reveals, bags of cement for 55 cents, or two-by-four spruce boards for 3.5 cents a foot. Nor is there a molderman replicating custom moldings, selecting his tools from more than 2,000 specialized knives, as he did at the turn of the century.

But there remains the dedicated staff, some 100 people in all. And almost any product desired can be found at J.E. Smith & Co.

CHECKMARK OFFICE SUPPLY, INC.

look, needs, and budget, but also a total concept that encompasses the entire interior and includes such components as carpentry, window treatments, partitions, and shelving.

Checkmark has clearly made its mark in the greater Waterbury region. The firm originally started out in an 800-square-foot building, soon expanding and relocating to a 7,000-square-foot building, and fi-

Checkmark Office Supply, located at 44 Chase River Road, is a commercial distributor of office supplies and equipment in the greater Waterbury area. More than 25,000 items are readily available.

As each new day dawns in Waterbury, it's business as usual, thanks to Checkmark Office Supply, Inc., which furnishes many of the Brass City area offices with essentials from adding machine rolls to fully-outfitted offices.

The company is located at 44 Chase River Road, in a modern 20,000-square-foot building that includes a 3,000-square-foot showroom.

It is a commercial distributor of office supplies and equipment in the greater Waterbury area, basically serving customers in a 20-mile radius of the city. Many area banks, hospitals, colleges, offices, and industries are valued Checkmark customers.

Through the years the firm has expanded its product lines to more than 25,000 items. And if Checkmark doesn't have it, it will arrange to obtain it.

Checkmark was founded in 1975 by Anthony Teta, who has more than 30 years' experience in the office supply business. At Checkmark, a customer's business needs are foremost. The company slogan is: "Your business is most appreciated, and we will endeavor to thank you with prompt service and quality merchandise at a fair price."

Service, quality, and value are the hallmarks of Checkmark. The company prides itself on maintain-

ing an organization that is knowledgeable in the product lines it offers. All together, the staff of 22 brings more than 150 years of experience and expertise to Checkmark customers.

In order to provide the most efficient service, the company is highly computerized, with orders tracked by computer. In addition, orders can be placed by customers around the clock using a FAX machine. The company offers free delivery and, in most cases, free installation.

Checkmark also offers design capabilities, not only furniture and office supplies that fit a customer's

nally, in 1984, to its present site. The building was designed by Teta and his staff to include a showroom as well as a large warehouse, and it is conveniently located just minutes away from Route 8.

Checkmark Office Supply, Inc., has a strong commitment to Waterbury. "It's my hometown," Teta says, "and we're here to stay. Our company is built on service before and after the sale.

"As Waterbury continues to grow, we will grow with the need and support it in every way by making the products that it needs available, and by seeing that the future needs are anticipated."

THE STARBUCK SPRAGUE COMPANY

Starbuck Sprague sounds like the name of a space explorer setting out to find the secret of all the sky's mysterious lights. In actuality, he was a businessman with two feet firmly planted on the ground but fascinated with the lights of this world. In 1927 he founded the firm that bears his name, The Starbuck Sprague Company, an electrical supplies distributor.

The business was acquired in 1978 by Helmuth W. Schultze, and in the ensuing decade Schultze guided its growth to the point where it has become one of Connecticut's largest sources of electrical supplies and lighting

The Starbuck Sprague Company's new home at 737 Bank Street was completed in 1986.

equipment. In 10 years the company's sales volume doubled almost three times, increasing from $2 million to $15 million, and the roster of employees more than tripled from 20 to 65 full-time workers.

The firm has also broadened and diversified its product lines but continues its traditional business of serving industry, business, construction, builders, and electricians with a wide range of electrical supplies that ranges from fuses to fittings, from switches to speed controls, from transformers to tools.

The company has added an extensive residential lighting area that includes a modern, 5,600-square-foot showroom, one of the largest in Connecticut. It features traditional and contemporary lighting fix-

tures, including track, recessed, decorative, outdoor, incandescent, and fluorescent lighting. The showroom is staffed by highly qualified employees who are especially trained to help customers make their selections from a functional and design standpoint.

Starbuck Sprague also specializes in commercial lighting, and the firm's professionally trained personnel provide assistance that includes complete lighting layouts to architects, specifiers, and builders for factories, offices, condominiums, schools, playgrounds, gymnasiums, production lines, and parking lots. Such personnel are qualified to perform all necessary lighting calculations and to determine the proper selections for such interior and exterior lighting, including security lighting.

Factory automation equipment, primarily manufactured by the Allen-Bradley Company, is another major product area. This new technology includes such devices as programmable controllers, drives, motor controls, and limit switches. Starbuck Sprague offers technical expertise in this area as well as a training facility, complete with hands-on demonstrations for

The fixtures in the lighting showroom represent all styles and types to meet customer needs.

An extensive inventory of electrical supplies can be seen by customers at the sales counter.

customers.

The Starbuck Sprague Company offers high-level personalized service at its new 40,000-square-foot facility at 737 Bank Street, which is open to the public. Therein awaits the special breed of Starbuck Sprague service, whether the customer is an industrialist wanting to increase productivity, an architect seeking lighting for a condominium complex, an electrician looking for a particular fitting, or a customer looking for a lamp.

Photo by Barry Rabinowitz

Photo by Georgia Sheron

Patrons

The following individuals, companies, and organizations have made a valuable commitment to the quality of this publication. Windsor Publications and the Greater Waterbury Chamber of Commerce and the Waterbury Convention and Visitors Commission gratefully acknowledge their participation in *Greater Waterbury: A Region Reborn.*

Airpax Company, A Division of North American Philips Corp.*
American Chemical & Refining Co., Inc.*
Anamet Inc.*
Bank of Boston Connecticut*
Bank of Waterbury*
Bristol Babcock Inc.*
Buell Industries, Inc.*
Carmody & Torrance*
Jaci Carroll Personnel Services, Inc.*
Centerbank*
Checkmark Office Supply, Inc.*
Cipriano & Associates*
The Connecticut Bank and Trust Company*
Connecticut Factors, Inc.*
Drubner Industrials*
The Dumouchel Paper Co.
The Eastern Company*
Erickson Metals Corporation*
Errichetti Associates*
G. Fox & Co.
Gager, Henry & Narkis*
General DataComm Industries*
Heritage Development Group, Inc.*
Hubbard-Hall Inc.*

Keeler & Long, Inc.*
Lenkowski, Lonergan & Co.*
Lewis Electronic Instrumentation Division/Colt*
MacDermid Incorporated*
F.B. Mattson Company, Inc.*
Northeast Utilities*
The Platt Brothers & Co.*
Post College*
Public Higher Education in Waterbury*
Risdon Corporation*
St. Mary's Hospital*
H.D. Segur, Inc.*
The Siemon Company*
J.E. Smith & Co.*
The Starbuck Sprague Company*
Summit Corporation of America*
The Taft School*
Tech Systems, Division of Datron Inc.*
Timex*
Torrington Supply Co., Inc.*
Truelove & Maclean Inc.*
Unisys*
United Electrical Contractors, Inc.*
Veeco Inc.*
Waterbury Development Agency*
Waterbury Hospital Health Center*
The Waterbury Republican and American*
WTXX-TV Channel 20*

*Participants in The Region's Enterprises, *Greater Waterbury: A Region Reborn.* The profiles of these companies and organizations appear in Part Two, beginning on page 142.

ANTIQUES
AND USED FURNITURE   Tel: 755-1840

OPEN

Photo by Georgia Sheron

Bibliography

Anderson, Joseph, *The Town and City of Waterbury,* 3 vols., New Haven, 1896.

Bassett, Homer F., *Waterbury and Her Industries,* Lithotype Printing and Publishing Co., Gardner, Mass., 1887.

Beach, Joseph Perkins, *History of Cheshire, Connecticut, from 1694 to 1840,* Lady Fenwick Chapter D.A.R., Cheshire, 1912.

Bronson, Henry, *Waterbury, Connecticut,* Bronson Brothers, Waterbury, 1858.

Brown, Edwin R., *Old Historic Homes of Cheshire, Connecticut,* New Haven, 1895.

Cathren, William, *History of Ancient Woodbury, Connecticut,* 3 vols., Bronson Brothers, Waterbury, 1854.

Gangloff, Rosa F., *The Story of Thomaston: Its Origin and Development,* Waterbury, 1975.

Green, Constance McL., *History of Naugatuck, Connecticut,* Naugatuck, Conn., 1948.

Litchfield, Norman and Sabina Connolly Hoyt, *History of the Town of Oxford,* 1960.

Maloney, Cornelius, et al., *Waterbury 1674-1974, A Pictorial History,* Pequot Press, Chester, Conn., 1974.

Orcutt, the Rev. Samuel, *History of the Town of Wolcott,* Waterbury, 1874.

Pape, W.J., *History of Waterbury and the Naugatuck Valley,* S.J. Clarke, Chicago, 1918.

Rockey, J.L., *History of New Haven County, Connecticut,* 2 vols., W.W. Preston & Co., New York, 1892.

Sharpe, W.C., *History of Oxford,* Seymour, Conn., 1885.

Stiles, Dan, *Town of Woodbury, Connecticut,* The Sugar Ball Press, Concord, New Hampshire, 1959.

Unattributed, *Art Work of Watertown, Waterbury and Naugatuck,* W.H. Parish Publishing Co., 1897.

Booklets, pamphlets

Brass Roots: A Short History of the Scovill Manufacturing Company, Mattatuck Historical Society, 1952.

Cowdell, Nellie H., *A History of the Prospect Congregational Church,* 1948.

Haddon, Rawson W., *Strangers in Town: Comments by Visitors to Waterbury, 1770-1873,* Mattatuck Historical Society, 1944.

Kingsbury, Alice Eliza, *In Old Waterbury,* Mattatuck Historical Society, 1942.

Kingsbury, Frederick, J., *The Green,* a paper prepared and published in 1876.

Washburne, John H., *Wolcott, Connecticut, 175th Anniversary, 1796-1971,* Wolcott, 1971.

Woodbury, Connecticut: A New England Townscape, The Preservation Press, Washington, D.C., 1975.

Articles, addresses, programs, etc.

Americana Illustrated, v. xxxii, no. 1, pp. 7-48, Somerville, N.J., *Mattatuck of Yore—Waterbury of Today.*

Official Souvenir Programme: Old Home Celebration and Dedication of New City Hall, Old Home Committee, Waterbury, 1915.

Quinn, Elizabeth, *The Story of Waterbury, 1917-1938,* Waterbury Sunday Republican, June 14—September 6, 1953.

The 150th Anniversary of the founding of Watertown, Connecticut, Pageant Committee, Watertown, 1930.

Index

This book was set in ITC Garamand type and printed on 70 lb. Mead Enamel.
Printing and binding by Walsworth Publishing Company.